The Evolutionary Mind

The Evolutionary Mind

Conversations on Science, Imagination & Spirit

RUPERT SHELDRAKE
TERENCE MCKENNA
RALPH ABRAHAM

MONKFISH BOOK PUBLISHING COMPANY
RHINEBECK, NEW YORK

Monkfish Book Publishing Company
27 Lamoree Road
Rhinebeck, New York 12572

First published as *The Evolutionary Mind: Trialogues at the Edge of the Unthinkable* by Trialogue Press. Copyright © 1998 by Rupert Sheldrake, Terence McKenna and Ralph Abraham.

Revised Edition
Design by Georgia Dent
Printed in the United States of America

Library of Congress Catalogue-in-Publication Data

Sheldrake, Rupert.
    The Evolutionary Mind: Trialogues at the edge of the unthinkable
    by Rupert Sheldrake, Terence McKenna, and Ralph Abraham.
    xvi + 194pp. cm.
    ISBN 0-942344-13-8 (ppk.)(org. ed.), Monkfish edition: 0-9749359-7-2
1. Cosmology. 2. Panpsychism. 3. Consciousness. 4. Gaia hypothesis. 5. Chaotic behavior in systems. 6. Religion and Science — 1946.
I. McKenna, Terence K., 1946- . II. Sheldrake, Rupert. III. Title.

    98-90256 CIP

    10 9 8 7 6 5 4 3 2

CIP data for first edition. For updated CIP data, please contact the publisher:
Monkfish Book Publishing Company

Bulk purchase discounts for educational or promotional purposes are available. Contact the publisher for more information.

Monkfish Book Publishing Company
27 Lamoree Road
Rhinebeck, New York 12572
www.monkfishpublishing.com

In Memory of
Father Bede Griffiths

CONTENTS

PREFACE

We became firm friends when we first met in 1982, in California, and met for discussions and conversation at regular intervals, both in the United States and in England until Terence's death on April 3rd, 2000.

Most of our time together was spent talking, trying out ideas, arguing, speculating, and enjoying each other's company. Our professional interests and backgrounds were very different. Ralph is a chaos mathematician and pioneer in the field of computer graphics; Terence, a psychedelic explorer, ethnopharmacologist, and theorist of time; and Rupert, a controversial biologist, best known for his hypothesis of morphic resonance, the idea that there is an inherent memory in nature.

Soon we found that these three-way discussions, which we call "Trialogues," were especially stimulating and fruitful, at least for ourselves. We had no thought of them being anything other than private meetings of friends. But after some six years of these informal conversations, Nancy Lunney, of the Esalen Institute, in Big Sur, California, asked us to lead a weekend workshop together. As a consequence, our trialogues emerged into the public domain in September 1989. These discussions, together with others we held at Esalen in private over the next two years, formed the ten chapters of our book, *Chaos, Creativity, and Cosmic Consciousness*, published in 2001 (first published in 1992 as *Trialogues at the Edge of the West*).

We have called this book *The Evolutionary Mind: Conversations on Science, Imagination and Spirit* because this title best summarizes the common themes of our discussions about the evolutionary mind. They are strongly influenced by the idea of the evolution of life, science, technology, culture, and indeed the entire cosmos. Our conversations are also influenced by the prospects for a greatly enlarged understanding of mind, expansion of experience and the transformation of consciousness beyond anything we presently conceive.

The trialogues in this book took place over several years and in several places: at the Esalen Institute, California; at Hazewood House, in the Devon countryside, in the West of England; at Terence's rainforest retreat on the Big Island of Hawaii, on the slopes of the volcano Mauna Loa; at the University of California at Santa Cruz and at Ralph's home, in the redwoods near the university.

An earlier version of this book called *The Evolutionary Mind: Trialogues at the Edge of the Unthinkable* was published by Trialogue Press, Santa Cruz, in 1998. The present book replaces this earlier version, which has been revised, updated and includes two new trialogues.

As always, we are very grateful to Becky Luening of Wordrhythm for the accuracy of her transcriptions, and to Paul Herbert for the gift of his recordings. We are indebted to Nancy Kaye Lunney and the Esalen Institute for hospitality in 1992, to the University of California at Santa Cruz for hospitality in 1998 and to David Jay Brown for his editing of the 1998 transcripts.

Rupert Sheldrake, London
Ralph Abraham, Santa Cruz

November, 2004

POSTSCRIPT TO PREFACE

My brother Terence McKenna, departed the corporeal plane in the spring of 2000. The rest of us remain stuck here, circumscribed by the limitations of space and time. For those who admired Terence's ideas, and especially, for those who admired the intellectual synergies that emerged out of the mind-play and conversations of these old and excellent friends, and manifested in the world as the trialogues, this book, likely to be the last published edition in the trialogues series, emerges as a special gift. The trialogues reflect the contributions, conversations, arguments and intellectual riffs of three brilliant minds, each a brilliant intellect, each widely versed in diverse aspects of science, art, philosophy, and esoteric lore, each freely bringing unique insights and perspectives to their free-wheeling discussions. The trialogues are a jam-session of the mind, an intellectual moveable feast, an on-going conversation that began over twenty years ago and remains as lively and relevant today as it ever was. Sadly, Terence had to leave the conversation a little earlier than planned. But the appearance of this book of trialogues at this critical historical juncture, while ever more dark and sinister forces cast their shadow over what we thought was to be the shining New Millennium, is a reaffirmation of the potency of the optimistic vision that the trialogues express. It is the same optimistic vision that Terence articulated so consistently in his teachings and writings. I would like to think that he would be very pleased to know that the message still resonates, twenty years after the conversation started and five years since he left the stage. We may think that we have witnessed much that would have been "unthinkable" just a few short years ago. The message of this new edition, which Terence would have heartily endorsed, is: just wait! You ain't seen nothing yet!

Dennis McKenna, Iquitos, Peru

November, 2004

But then something amazing happened about fifty thousand years ago—the beginnings of art, such as paintings in caves. This had nothing to do with a sudden increase in brain size. Our ancestors already had brain sizes roughly the same as ours today. Yet a hundred thousand years ago they were not thinking up Einstein's equations, or building jet aircraft, or writing computer programs. What happened?

CHAPTER 1

THE EVOLUTIONARY MIND

Rupert Sheldrake: In the 1990s psychologists discovered Darwin and so, many of them took up evolutionary psychology. I keep meeting psychologists who speak to me with the enthusiasm and bright eyes of new converts, as though they've seen the light. As a biologist, I wonder why they didn't discover Darwin a long time ago. After all, Darwin opened up the field of evolutionary psychology with his book *The Expression of the Emotions in Man and Animals*. There was much speculation at the end of the nineteenth century about the evolution of consciousness. However, in the twentieth century academic psychology got obsessed in behaviorism, with rats in cages pushing levers. Then cognitive psychology and computer models of neuroprocessing took over, and these left little space for evolutionary theorizing. So in affect psychologists have come rather late to evolutionary speculation.

Sociobiologists and evolutionary psychologists have given themselves permission to speculate about the evolution of the mind by thinking in terms of selfish genes. They feel that if they're talking about selfish genes it's somehow scientific. This kind of discussion is epitomized in Steven Pinker's book *How the Mind Works*, which is based on the idea that human behavior is determined by genes, and there's a gene for everything. In theoretical terms, he worked out what the selfish behavior of the genes would lead us to expect. Unfortunately, his conclusions were neither deep nor surprising.

I was at a lecture Pinker gave at the London School of Economics, which met with considerable skepticism. Someone asked him, "Just give us one clear and important idea you've been able to deduce from selfish theory." He replied that because females have only one or two eggs at a time, they are a rare and precious resource that needs conserving, whereas males produce millions of sperm. So on the basis of neo-Darwinian principles he deduced that women would tend to seek high status males and want to stay with them, while men would tend to be promiscuous in order to spread selfish genes more freely. There was an air of disappointment in the lecture hall, and somebody said, "Is that all? Surely we knew that already."

The theories of evolutionary psychology are speculative since we don't really know what happened in the past. Many of them are "just-so" stories, rather like Kipling's account of how the leopard got its spots. But several rather interesting ideas have come up.

A book by the British archaeologist Stephen Mithen, The *Prehistory of the Mind* brings together a wealth of evidence from the fossil record, archaeology, the study of primate behavior and from child psychology. He discusses what's happened in human minds during the three-and-a-half million years of human evolution before recorded history began. The first upright walking hominids, who were our precursors are now believed to have emerged in Africa over three-and-a-half million years ago. Three-and-a-half million years of human history went on before we had the records from the great civilizations. The domestication of animals and the agricultural revolution occurred around ten thousand years ago. The first civilizations occurred about five, maybe seven, thousand years ago. Industrialization began only around two or three hundred years ago. But for the vast majority of human history, people were living in a quite different way. It is a reasonable supposition that a great deal of our psychology was being shaped by this enormously long period about which we know so little.

What Mithen points out is that, although we don't know what the early hominids thought about or how they worked, they must have had several different kinds of intelligence, like a kind of mental Swiss Army knife. Our ancestors must have had a social intelligence because they lived in social groups. We know from studies of chimpanzees and other social primates that there are very subtle interactions within the group-like combinations of dominant and cooperative interactions. Getting it right requires a kind of intelligence with regard to how other members of the group are going to react, and what's considered appropriate behavior. Since all social animals must utilize some kind of social intelligence, we can reasonably assume that our hominid ancestors had a social intelligence enabling them to live and work together in social groups.

In addition, they had a technical intelligence that enabled them to make tools, and maybe other things, such as fibers and strings, which haven't left traces in the archaeological record. They also must have had a knack for natural historical intelligence; because living as hunter-gatherers, they would not have survived for long unless they knew what to hunt, how to hunt it, and what the habits of the animals were that they were hunting. They had to know what to gather, where to gather it, and what plants are good to eat or have value as herbs.

Then, at some stage, they began to talk, so they must have had a linguistic intelligence although we don't know when language began. Some people put it at fifty thousand years ago, while others think it began much earlier, but nobody really knows. Language leaves no fossil traces.

But then something amazing happened about fifty thousand years ago—the beginnings of art, such as paintings in caves. This had nothing to do with a sudden increase in brain size. Our ancestors already had brain sizes roughly the same as ours today. Yet a hundred thousand years ago they were not thinking up Einstein's equations, or building jet aircraft, or writing computer programs. The development of current brain size is not the reason that there's been an explosion of human culture today. Something else was going on with those brains, and we haven't a clue what it was. What happened? What enabled these different kinds of intelligence to give rise to the agricultural revolution and modern humanity? Mithen's hypothesis is that about fifty thousand years ago some crucial transition occurred whereby these previously separate intelligences somehow came together, cross-fertilized each other, and produced the beginnings of characteristically human mentality. The connection of social and technical intelligence meant that people started using technical skills for making things such as jewelry, ornaments, and gravestones.

The mixing of technical and natural historical intelligence led to a great improvement in hunting technologies and weapons—axes, spearheads, arrowheads, and so on. The merging of social and natural historical intelligence led to a kind of mythic view of animals in the natural world, which we find in all cultures around the world today. Combining these types of intelligence with linguistic intelligence produced a whole burst of mental development.

Mithen compares this process to changes in cathedral architecture. A Romanesque cathedral built around 1100 AD has side chapels almost sealed off from each other with no interaction, whereas the great Gothic cathedrals are more open, with the different spaces intercommunicating. He thinks this transition fifty thousand years ago was associated with the origin of religion, and it seems to have been based on a sense of human connection not just with the earth, but with the heavens.

I asked Mithen how he understood this happened, especially given his chosen metaphor of the cathedral. I asked him, "Do you think there really was a breakthrough from some extraterrestrial intelligence into the human realm at that stage, since all your evidence points to it?"

He said, "Of course not! That's impossible!"

So I asked, "How do you know it's impossible, since everybody all around the world, according to your own evidence, seems to have undergone this transition? It seems to have shaped human mentality as we know it."

"Ah yes," he said, "The very fact that everyone believes it shows that this is an incredibly persistent illusion."

"Surely," I said, "You can have things that are true which are persistent too." He admitted, in the end, it was just a matter of opinion. His opinion was that no nonhuman higher forms of consciousness existed. But everything he said points to some breakthrough to another realm of consciousness around fifty thousand years ago, something that happened within human groups all around the earth. Some people might like to interpret that in terms of visits from aliens in spaceships. But there are many other ways of thinking about it, and I can guess that Terence will be able to suggest at least one—the discovery of magic mushrooms.

There's another speculation about the past that I find particularly interesting. Barbara Ehrenreich in her book *Blood Rites* completely changed around my idea of human prehistory. What she shows is that our image of man-the-hunter striding forth about three million years ago onto the African Savannah is implausible. Human beings were small. They couldn't run very fast. They weren't particularly strong. Their tools were extremely primitive. It's much more likely that, for most of human history, it was man-the-hunted.

In fact, many of the bones of early hominids show the scratches and tooth marks of large cats. Human beings were on the African Savannah with lots of game, but also with big predators. They were extremely vulnerable, and a great deal of human mentality, she argues, was shaped by millions of years of being preyed on. It wasn't until about fifty thousand years ago that there was an improvement in hunting technologies, whereby human beings could indeed become more effective hunters.

She shows that this sheds light on many religious traditions in which there's the idea of a sacrificial victim. When a predator approaches a herd of wildebeests or baboons, they usually attack isolated members of a group—the old, the young, or sometimes the young males who are defending the periphery of the group. They get killed first. After they've killed one and start eating it, the rest of the group can relax. They sometimes stand around and watch the predator eating the prey. When the predators have a victim, they are not interested in the rest of the group. So one member of the group dies, and the others are safe for a while. This is a simple fact of predation.

Ehrenreich shows that this pattern, a sacrificial victim that dies for the sake of the rest, is deeply embedded in our consciousness as an archetypal pattern. She points out that most of the early gods and goddesses were seen as carnivores, for example Horus, the hawk god of Egypt. Even Jehovah is a carnivore. In the story of Cain and Abel, Cain is a farmer who offers the fruit of the earth to God as a sacrifice, and Abel is a herder who offers a sheep (Gen. 4. 2-10). God prefers Abel's offering. God likes meat more than produce, so Cain kills Abel. He's jealous.

Ehrenreich then points out that whole nations identify with predators, and in wars the whole nation becomes like a predator. The symbol of England and many other countries is the lion; the symbol of the United States, the eagle. All around the world predatory animals are national emblems.

I think Ehrenreich's insights are particularly interesting because they show that so much of our mythology, religious structure, and fears are related to this long period of being preyed on. The nightmares of young children in modern cities like New York are not about child molesters or being run over by cars; they're about being eaten by monsters and wild animals.

Stephen Mithen's and Barbara Ehrenreich's ideas about early human history have important implications for our collective memories. I would think of them as collective memories that we inherit by morphic resonance. Jung would call them archetypes in the collective unconscious. Our memories, those things that are built into our past, shape the way that our minds are today, in ways that we're largely unaware of. This is because our usual study of history begins with the civilizations of the Near East, Egypt, Greece and Rome. It leaves out the previous three-and-a-half million years of human history, a time that has really done so much to shape our evolutionary nature and therefore, conditions the way we respond to each other today and in the future.

Terence McKenna: First of all, let's assume that I've responded to this with the usual rap about diet and mushrooms. In trying to greater understand this moment of transition or breakthrough fifty thousand years ago, I come very close to what Rupert's just been discussing. I can't help but notice that a successful predator must think like its prey, that there is this peculiar intellectual symbiosis that goes on between the predator and the prey. I think that top carnivores, like hunting cats, internalize the behaviors of their prey.

At the very dawn of the evolutionary emergence of mind, the central human figure in that equation is the shaman. At the high Paleolithic stage, the shaman is essentially a kind of sanctioned psychotic. In other words, shamans are able to move into states of mind so extreme that their immediate social efficacy is arguable. What I mean is that the shaman is a person, a designated member of the social group, who can mentally change into an animal. The shaman can become so animal-like that other members of the social group are appalled and draw back. So, in a weird way, at this fractal boundary where human consciousness emerges, the first human consciousness was not human at all. It was a human ability to model effectively the thinking processes of other predators.

Ralph Abraham: With mathematical models.

TM: Yes, with mathematical models and precision. So when we're talking about hunting, we're talking about strategic thinking, which always involved bifurcating trees of choice. If we go to the water hole at dawn, perhaps we can make a kill. If we leave the women and children, take food, and go in this direction several days, perhaps we will make a kill. Perhaps not. Perhaps by abandoning the women and the children we will undercut our gene pool and return to catastrophe

Strategic thinking requires the ability to contemplate possibilities that are not immediately present. In other words, there's a kind of time-binding function here. So I'm really not so much posing a question to Rupert as adumbrating what he said. This is where it all comes together, in this very complicated relationship between fear, expectation, strategizing, and the imagination. The two areas where I'm sure we spent a great deal of time studying these bifurcating trees of possibility were in the food gathering and hunting domain, and then in the sexual domain, which today we call erotic fantasy. But in the high Paleolithic, erotic fantasy was rather closely welded to where our genes went and how our biological propagation proceeded.

So whatever the causal mechanism was—the stimulation of psilocybin or modeling the behavior of the top predators that we competed with—the domain in which the change was born, and in which we will live until we leave the body behind us, is the domain of the imagination. This is what we created that is uniquely human, and that has defined us ever since. When our discussions look more into the future, I think we will see that as the imagination has been our past, and the cradle of our humanness, so it also is the domain in which our trans-human metamorphosis will occur.

RA: As far as I can see, this is like dancing around an intellectual black hole. The question of what caused the bifurcation in the evolution of consciousness or culture fifty thousand years ago is of interest to us because we're in one now. Rupert proposed that you would, of course, answer psilocybin mushroom among the clans of Africa.

TM: And the need to think strategically.

RA: But not only was this need a constant throughout the three-and-a-half million year evolution of hominids, but it was also present in apes, swarming bees, schooling fish and many other animals. What was it then, if anything, that happened fifty thousand years ago? There's a dichotomy of two different views about this bifurcation: the divine intervention one, and the physiological, random mutation, natural selection one. In this dichotomy we see Rupert and Terence opposed. Terence believes the eating of psilocybin mushrooms is a purely material explanation, right? It requires no recourse to a divine intervention in the field by way of angels or dreams. You use the word imagination.

TM: Rupert's not suggesting a little divine intervention. He's just speaking metaphorically.

RS: I'm speaking literally. It's Mithen who's speaking metaphorically. One of the things we have to explain is that religion, a relationship that is beyond the human realm of consciousness, is found in every human culture today. One way or another every culture speaks of a world of spirits, angels, or gods. But to explain the universal distribution of this aspect of traditional human thinking requires that, at some stage in the past, there has been an awareness of other realms of consciousness. This is not incompatible with psilocybin or any other drug hypothesis, because psychedelics might have kick-started this connection with other realms of consciousness.

If we recognize that shaman cultures and all other cultures and other kinds of conscious entities beyond the human level—some in animal forms and some in other forms— in some stage in the past experienced these other realms of consciousness, whatever they are. Not just metaphors, not just archetypes in the collective mind, but forms of consciousness that might well be actually out there.

TM: In trying to think conservatively about the possibility of a nonhuman local intelligence, it seems to me that Nature herself presents intelligence. The understanding of Nature is the understanding of complex integrated systems of such complexity that denying them consciousness is just a reluctance of the reductionist mind. For anyone not burdened by that prejudice, it's self-evident that Nature is alive, cognizant, responding.

It's interesting that really all we can agree upon here is that the time frame is roughly fifty thousand years. So a whole bunch of things are triangulating on that moment. One could say, as I've argued, that it was the eating of psilocybin mushrooms. You could make a more general statement and say that was the subset of the consequence of an omnivorous diet.

RA: Where were these mushrooms a hundred thousand years ago?

TM: The way I think about it is there was an incremental involvement that had punctuated breakthroughs in it. In other words, the slow meeting of mind, mushroom, social complexity, acoustical abilities linked to neurophysiological states didn't just smoothly proceed. It all came together, but then at a certain point it jelled, and this is the fifty-thousand-year point where social understanding, technology, linguistic repertoires, and depth of diet all came together.

RA: You're clinging to this material stuff.

TM: There will be material stuff even if you believe that angels descended from on high.

The invention of writing nine thousand years ago was an enormous breakthrough. But all of these things proceed out of the further integration and complexification of the nervous system in connection with the function of the imagination.

RA: I can't believe that you're presenting yourself as a conventional, materialist, evolutionary theorist.

TM: With the mushroom theory, you can always just say our human ancestors encountered the mushroom and then it proceeded from there. But you can go one step back and ask who placed the mushroom in their path?

RA: Oh, I can give you a hand there. There was the preceding civilization of Lemurians. They died out because they had poisoned the environment with toxic chemicals and created global climate warming. This resulted in a drying of the Sahara desert, from which sprung forth a bloom of psychedelic mushrooms that had been hiding under the surface previously because it was too wet.

TM: The loud hum I hear is William of Ockham spinning in his grave.

RA: I see. You think that DNA and the expression of genes is a simpler explanation than a divine intervention.

TM: I think the DNA is divine.

RA: Ah!

TM: Escape! Rupert, what do you, as the middle man, think?

RS: I can't quite get your position, Terence, because the new hard-nosed skeptic that you're revealing to us here is another personality that doesn't seem to fit too well with the Terence

McKenna of nonhuman entities and self-transforming machine elves. Are these other kinds of consciousness, other forms of entity just inside our brains, appearing in relation to pharmacologically induced states of mind? The idea that they're out there seems to me an integral part of most of what I've heard you say over many years.

TM: I think the key thing is not to concentrate on materialist versus nonmaterialist explanations. Rather, it is to realize that the new vision of nature is not as matter or energy, but as information, and information is expressed in the DNA. It's expressed epigenetically in culture. What's happening is that information was running itself on a primate platform, but evolving according to its own agenda. In a sense we have a symbiotic relationship to a nonmaterial being which we call language. We think it's ours, and we think we control it. This isn't what's happening. It's running itself. It's time-sharing a primate nervous system, and evolving toward its own conclusions.

RS: The discussion so far has been remarkably earth-bound. What if information and consciousness are not confined to this planet? Other parts of the universe—stars, suns, and galaxies—may be conscious. If so, it becomes very likely that, at some stage, minds on earth could somehow link to those higher forms of consciousness.

Who knows how? Maybe by some kind of telepathy. But if there was a direct connection at some stage between human consciousness and other forms of consciousness in the universe, then when that contact was established there would have been a big transition. It could have been stimulated by drugs, or by other means. But however it happened, this connection with other forms of consciousness would have transformed human nature.

RA: Terence, can I remind you of a quotation from the front pages of your first book? You speculated that mushroom spores are intergalactic travelers, that they have a hard case impervious to ultraviolet rays which enables them to float on the galactic wind from planetary system to planetary system, bringing us linguistic communications from other life forms, including immaterial life forms that they've been in conversation with in the past. I think this is an approximate summary of your premise.

TM: But notice how materialist and space-and-time bound that hypothesis is. I could agree with everything Rupert said. I think now our intellectual tool-kit has been enriched by the virtual confirmation of the idea that there is a Bell-type, nonlocal aspect to the universe, as in quantum entanglement. So I do think we're in contact with all intelligence in the universe through quantum nonlocal connections. But that means that this connection has no history. It has always been there complete and entire. So while there is a sense of progressing toward it, or it's erupting through into normal earthbound affairs, it is not because someone in the Andromeda galaxy makes a decision, "Now we will reveal ourselves to the earthlings." It's that the antennae system and the nervous system of the earthlings evolved to a point that suddenly this connection became self-evident.

RA: Now we're coming to the question for the first time in the enlarged context, where which we have, not only all space, but all time informing us. And here I may remind you of Father Bede's letter (see Chapter 11), where he challenges us to consider the mystical element, which he describes, more or less, in the language of David Bohm's implicate order—that all time and space somehow exist as an interconnected ball of intelligence.

Let's just assume that the science of our colleagues is more or less a true story of evolution. There was a change and language did come upon us at a certain moment. Before that moment we didn't speak; afterward we did. So the question arises: How could it be, with or without divine intervention, that there is this progress in human intelligence, culture, capability, tool-using, and exponential population growth, that it is correlated without any causal implication with the descent of the novelty wave?

TM: Novelty Theory would just say the universe is a complexity-conserving engine. Whatever complexity it achieves, by any means, it makes that the platform for a further thrust into deeper complexity.

RA: Because the morphic field never forgets.

TM: They forget a little. They can be set back, but they can never be set back to zero, and once they get out of the ditch, they always head back in the same direction, They have a vector field preference.

Then you mention David Bohm. His idea of emergent properties seems to achieve the same end as novelty theory.

He simply says that when you complexify a system, new properties will emerge suddenly and unexpectedly that couldn't have been predicted. Both Emergence Theory and Novelty Theory predict that the universe would proceed along the line of complexification of morphogenetic expression, density of connectivity, and all the things that retard entropy and give rise to the complex, nonentropic, ordered, apparently teleologically-informed cosmos that we're in.

RA: Now we see that you've revealed a kind of evolutionary theory as a cosmological hypothesis. This is a theological position, basically that there is timeless, implicate order. According to this position there is life on planet Earth, and in the rest of the universe, which evolves according to this theoretical rule by an increase of complexity. When something is revealed there's a development. It's not forgotten; it builds upon that. This mystical unity, while knowing all, is not telling all, but revealing gradually—because that's just the law of life, as we know it. Is that what you're saying?

TM: From my point of view, the only difference between the morphic field that Rupert has enthusiastically proposed, and the ideas of my Novelty Theory is for me it's pulled from the future. For Rupert it's pushed from the past. What you get at the end of the day is the same thing. It's just a matter of preference and how much of orthodoxy you want to grind against. The phobia against *telos*—against ends, goals or purposes—is an artifact of nineteenth century rationalism and that doesn't go very deep. You described the complexification of the universe as self-evident, and I believe it is self-evident. The failure of science to address this is what makes it so frustrating.

RS: But the problem with the Emergence Theory is that it's still very earthbound. There has obviously been a major emergence of complexity in human conscious. There's also been a huge emergence of complexity in the Amazon and the Malaysian rain forests, arguably far greater than anything we've achieved through technology—millions of species of beetles, plants and so forth. But it seems to me that, long before all these things happened on earth, there is the possibility of much higher levels of consciousness outside the earth. As you know, I like the idea that the sun and stars are conscious. When we're talking about the emergence of higher consciousness in human beings, it's not as if for the first time in the universe some higher level of consciousness emerged. It could be that for the first time in the history of the solar system the biologically-based minds have contacted a source of much greater intelligence which exists out there. Because the sun, stars, and galaxies may be conscious, you don't need to go straight beyond the universe to the divine mind.

Of course, traditional views of spirits and angels tell us that there are innumerable levels of intelligence beyond our own. So we don't necessarily have to have the idea that it all happened and emerged on earth through a complexification. We may have reached a point where a spark passed between a higher consciousness and a human one, perhaps in the throes of a mind-boggling mushroom trip. But whatever happens, somehow a connection was established. It seems to me that this hypothesis has a great advantage in actually accounting for what's believed all around the world, namely that there is some connection between human intelligence and intelligences in the sky.

TM: I'm friendlier to this idea of non-biologically based forms of consciousness than I was the last time we talked. I now think that wherever there is a sufficiently complex informational environment, the functions of life—self-replication, mutation, adaptation, —can go on. But, obviously, most of the intelligence in the universe would be utterly incomprehensible to us because it is so different.

We're virtually converting the entire hologram of possible intelligence in the universe, but the reason our fantasies of angels and aliens give us hominids with binocular vision who use acoustical speech—in other words, creatures very similar to ourselves—is because we can only recognize what is familiar in this universal information field. So we sail right past the star mind, the galaxy mind, to communicate with a race of winged hominids around Delta Cephei, simply because they are enough like us that we can grok our possibility of a relationship.

RA: It seems to me that this is just begging the question in the traditional cheap fashion. I'm all in favor of celestial intelligence. In fact, I could even entertain a conversation with a Pleiad. I don't mind. But we started with the problem of the evolution of consciousness. The question of the evolution of progress is our ultimate question. Now if our view is local to planet Earth, we can say that bolts from the blue are teaching us, and meddling celestial intelligences are reaching down to us. They pretend to be Bell and tell us Bell's Theorem. They give us mushrooms. They pretend to be sent from the solar wind or whatever. But where do they come from? The evolutionary origin is transferred onto another, more remote place. Now, as I understand Rupert's idea of the morphic fields, these other places are also in evolution and the whole system is in co-evolution. That is an attempt—I think one of the first ones in the history of intelligent discourse on this subject—to get rid of the hypothesis of timeless truth.

TM: But if you get rid of that hypothesis you have a whole bunch of weird problems. For example, then you have to talk about the speed of propagation of novelty or morphic fields. Then you're slammed to the wall because you have to either come up with a number, which you fit into a mathematical architecture, or you say that it's instantaneous, which returns you to this holistic, more metaphysical thing. You have a whole bunch of these kinds of problems, which I think, intuitively, make it too complicated.

RA: Let it be instantaneous. I think the whole question of time is, in fact, behind this problem. We have this idea about time, and then we're trying to talk about "timelessness." One way to eliminate this cognitive dissonance is to say there is no timelessness. It's all in co-evolution, and we're a little bit behind the evolution of the Pleiads. Then where does that come from? We're stuck with the problem. I think the attractor at the end of time that you talk about is, more or less, as beyond time as the intelligence that it informs. That nourishes the accumulation of complexity as we go along, apparently in time.

TM: I think the attractor is complete, in and of itself, in another dimension. The process of history and biological evolution is the process of growing complex enough to grow toward the thing and understand it.

RA: So then, is our process of growth nourished or not nourished by some flow of something that comes from this attractor at the end of time in another dimension?

TM: It contributes the trajectory of our approach. It defines the domain we are moving toward. What is given is that there shall be ever greater complexity. What is not given is how this complexity shall arrange itself, or what the final end state will be. It's a story that's being told as it unfolds. It's a game, one of the rules of which is that the rules can change.

RA: So the attractor at the end of the time then only has in it the simple rule of a board game: that the complexity is going to increase. How it's evolving, and stuff we can make up as we go along, all come later. Whatever natural selection approves of will then come to pass. Complexity will increase, that's the only rule. So, in fact, you agree that time is slowing down.

TM: Time is slowing down as the event potentially contained within any given moment exponentially expands. In other words, we're sort of in a situation of a spaceship falling into a black hole. From the point of view of a distant observer, the spaceship falls into the black hole. There's a flash of hard radiation, and the story is over. From the point of view of the people on the spaceship, the relativistic stretching of the time line means you fall forever and you never reach the conclusion. Time is not a tyranny. It is a relativistic medium subject to all kinds of plasticity. There are many ways out of any assumed corner we may paint ourselves into.

The nuts and bolts question posed in all of this is, "Can the psyche-delic state be visualized with technologies ranging from paint and brush to super computers?" I think it can.

I feel that part of our difficulty is our culture's rejection of math-ematics. Mathematics is essentially the marriage of Father Sky and Mother Earth. I've given my life work to understand this rela-tionship between the psychedelic and the mathematical vision.

CHAPTER 2

PSYCHEDELICS, COMPUTERS, AND VISUAL MATHEMATICS

Ralph Abraham: One day I was sitting in my office with my secretary, Nina, when there was a knock on the door. Nina introduced us; "This is a friend of a friend of mine, who wants to interview you." I was very busy with the telephone and the correspondence, so he came inside and I answered his questions without thinking. After a month or so, when a photographer arrived, I began to realize that I had given an interview for *Gentleman's Quarterly (GQ)* magazine. I called my children and asked them what was *GQ*—since they live in Hollywood and know about such things.

I was in Firenze, Italy when the magazine finally arrived on the stands. I was very proud that in spite of my style of dress, I had been the first one in our circle of family and friends to actually be photographed for *GQ*. But I was shocked to open the first page of the magazine, and see my picture occupying a large part of the first page in of the table of contents with the heading: "Abraham Sells Drugs to Mathematicians." There were some other insulting things in the interview that as far as I can remember, was largely fiction. I didn't mention it to anybody when I came back to California, and I was very pleased that nobody mentioned it. Nobody had noticed. There were one or two phone calls, and I realized that nobody after all reads *GQ*. If they do look at the pictures, they overlooked mine. I was safe after all at this dangerous pass.

Suddenly, my initial peace was disturbed by 100 phone calls in a single day asking what I thought of the article about me in the *San Francisco Examiner*, or the *San Jose Mercury News*. All the embers in the fire left by *GQ* had flamed up again in the pen of a journalist. A woman who writes a computer column for the *San Francisco Examiner* had received in her mailbox a copy of the *Gentleman's Quarterly* article, in which Timothy Leary was quoted as saying, "The Japanese go to Burma for teak, and they go to California for novelty and creativity. Everybody knows that California has this resource thanks to psychedelics." Then the article quoted me as the supplier for the scientific renaissance in the 1960s.

This columnist didn't believe what was asserted by Timothy Leary and others in the *GQ* article, that the computer revolution and the computer graphic innovations of California had been built upon a psychedelic foundation. She set out to prove this story false. She went to Siggraph, the largest gathering of computer graphic professionals in the world, where annually gather some 30,000 people who are vitally involved in the computer revolution. She thought she would set this heresy to rest by conducting a sample survey by beginning her interviews at the airport the minute she stepped off the plane. By the time she got back to her desk in San Francisco she'd talked to 180 important professionals in the computer graphic field, all of whom answered *yes* to the question, "Do you take psychedelics, and is this important in your work?" Her column, finally syndicated in a number of newspapers again, unfortunately, or kindly, remembered me.

Shortly after this second incident in my story, I was in Hollyhock, the Esalen of the far north, on Cortes Island in British Columbia, with Rupert and other friends. I had a kind of psychotic break in the night. I couldn't sleep and was consumed with a paranoid fantasy about this outing and what it would mean in my future career—the police at my door, whatever. I knew that my fears had blown up unnecessarily, but I needed someone to talk to. The person I knew best there was Rupert. He was very busy in counsel with various friends, but eventually I took Rupert aside and confided to him this secret and all my fears. His response, within a day or two, was to repeat the story to everybody in Canada, assuring me that it's good to be outed. I tried thinking positively about this episode, but when I came home I still felt nervous about it and said no to interviews from ABC News, the United Nations, and other people who called to check out this widely covered story. I did not then rise to the occasion, and so I've decided today, by popular request, to tell the truth.

It all began in 1967 when I was a professor of mathematics at Princeton, and one of my students turned me on to LSD. That led to my moving to California a year later, and meeting at UC Santa Cruz a chemistry graduate student who was doing his Ph.D. thesis on the synthesis of DMT (dimethyl tryptamine). He and I smoked up a large bottle of DMT in 1969, and that resulted in a kind of secret resolve, which swerved my career toward a search for the connections between mathematics and the experience of the Logos, or what Terence calls "the transcendent other." This is a hyperdimensional space full of meaning and wisdom and beauty, which feels more real than ordinary reality, and to which we have returned many times over the years, for instruction and pleasure. In the course of the next 20 years there were various steps I took to explore the connection between mathematics and the Logos.

About the time that the scientific community discovered chaos theory, and the chaos revolution began in 1978, I apprenticed myself to a neurophysiologist and tried to construct brain models made out of the basic objects of chaos theory. I built a vibrating fluid machine to visualize vibrations in transparent media, because I felt on the basis of direct experience that the Hindu metaphor of vibrations was important and valuable. I felt that we could learn more about consciousness, communication, resonance, and the emergence of form and pattern in the physical, biological, social and intellectual worlds, through actually watching vibrations in transparent media ordinarily invisible, and making them visible. I was inspired by Hans Jenny, an amateur scientist in Switzerland, a follower of Rudolf Steiner, who had built an ingenious gadget for visibly rendering patterns in transparent fluids.

About this time we discovered computer graphics in Santa Cruz, when the first affordable computer graphic terminals had appeared on the market. I started a project of teaching mathematics with computer graphics, and eventually tried to simulate the mathematical models for neurophysiology and for vibrating fluids, in computer programs with computer graphic displays. In this way evolved a new class of mathematical models called CDs, cellular dynamata. CDs are an especially appropriate mathematical object for modeling and trying to understand the brain, the mind, or the visionary experience. At the same time other mathematicians, some of whom may have been recipients of my gifts in the 1960s, began their own experiments with computer graphics in different places and began to make films.

Eventually, we were able to construct machines in Santa Cruz which could simulate these mathematical models I call CDs at a reasonable speed, first slowly, and then faster and faster. And in 1989, I had a fantastic experience at the NASA Goddard Space Flight Center in Maryland, where I was given access to at that time, the world's fastest super computer, the MPP, the Massively Parallel Processor. My CD model for the visual cortex had been programmed into this machine by the only person able to program it, and I was invited to come and view the result. Looking at the color screen of this super computer was like looking through the window at the future and seeing an excellent memory of a DMT vision, not only proceeding apace on the screen, but also going about 100 times faster than a human experience. Under the control of knobs, which I could turn at the terminal, we immediately recorded a video, which lasts for 10 minutes.To sum up my story, there is first of all, a twenty-year evolution from my first DMT vision in 1969, to my experience with the Massively Parallel Processor vision in 1989. Following this twenty-year evolution, and the recording of the video, the story with *GQ* and the interviews at Siggraph in the *San Francisco Examiner* appeared that essentially posed the question, "Have psychedelics had an influence in the evolution of science, mathematics, the computer revolution, computer graphics, and so on?"

Another event, in 1990, followed the publication of a paper in the *International Journal of Bifurcations and Chaos*, when an interesting article appeared in the monthly notices of the American Mathematical Society, the largest union of research mathematicians in the world. The article totally redefined mathematics, dropping numbers and geometrical spaces as relics of history, and adopting a new definition of mathematics as the study of space/time patterns. Mathematics has been reborn, and this rebirth is an outcome of both the computer revolution and the psychedelic revolution that took place concurrently, concomitantly, cooperatively, in the 1960s.

Redefining this material as an art medium, I gave a concert, played in real-time with a genuine super computer, in October 1992, in the Cathedral of Saint John the Divine, the largest Gothic cathedral in the world, in New York City.

We now come to our subject. I want to pose one or two questions, and read here one or two excerpts from some favorite books. We have to accept, I think, mathematics either in the new definition, or the old one. In the Renaissance cosmology of John Dee, mathematics is seen as the joint therapist of Father Sky and Mother Earth, or a kind of an intellectual, spiritual, elastic medium connecting up the heavenly realms and Gaia herself. That puts mathematics on the same level as the Logos, or the Holy Spirit. Let's consider that for the sake of discussion. Having seen mathematics as a language of space/time pattern, let me ask you this, Terence and Rupert: To what extent could the psychedelic vision of the Logos be externalized, either by verbal descriptions or by computer simulations, or by drawings of inspired visionary artists? On the other hand, in what ways could mathematical vision serve the spirit, and extend the mind? Is there a role, in other words, for this kind of thing in our main concerns? To give you a fast-forward toward the answer, let me read a couple of things from your writings.

First, from Terence's *Food of the Gods: The archaic revival is a clarion call to recover our birthright, however uncomfortable that may make us. It is a call to realize that life lived in the absence of the psychedelic experience, upon which primordial shamanism is based, is life trivialized, life denied! Life enslaved to the ego and its fear of dissolution in the mysterious matrix of feeling that is all around us. It is in the archaic revival that our transcendence of the historical dilemma actually lies. There is something more. It is now clear that the new developments in many areas including mind machine interfacing, pharmacology of the synthetic variety, and data storage imaging and retrieval techniques are coalescing into the potential for a truly demonic, or an angelic self-imaging of our culture.*

Our second passage is from Rupert's *The Rebirth of Nature: As soon as we allow ourselves to think of the world as alive, we recognize that a part of us knew this all along. It is like emerging from winter into spring. We can begin to reconnect our mental life with our own direct, intuitive experiences of nature. We can participate in the spirits of sacred places and times. We can see that we have much to learn from traditional societies who have never lost their sense of connection with the living world around them. We can acknowledge the animistic traditions of our ancestors, and we can begin to develop a richer understanding of human na-*

ture, shaped by a tradition and collective memory, linked to the earth and the heavens, related to all forms of life and consciously open to the creative power expressed in all evolution. We are reborn into a living world.

Terence McKenna: The nuts and bolts question posed in all of this is, "Can the psychedelic state be visualized with technologies ranging from paint and brush to super computers?" I think it can. I think it's not, in principle, mysterious. It may be fleeting, like the situation that follows upon the splitting of the atom. It may be remote. But it is in principle describable. It's a domain to be explored. It's simply a matter of paying attention, gaining inspiration, and gaining skill of technical execution.

RA: Any models that we can build, verbal, visual, or mathematical, are feeble compared to the experience itself. On the other hand, this experience is within all, and without all, and we are immersed in the spiritual world, so the tiniest resonance from the feeblest model may suffice to excite, as poetry excites emotion, spirit. The essence of communication is to have a compact representation of an experience that's infinitely complex. The representations have to be really simple. Representation restricted to verbal mode alone might be too feeble to excite by resonance, the similar state. Not every person is going to become a cephalopod. Not every person has the time to become a shaman. We need, however, a certain number of shamans in our culture to help to reconnect human society and the play in the sky. We need some kind of amplifying and communicating device between the few people who are our real shamans, let's say sacred artists of the future, and the mass society watching MTV. The question is, can these means be of use to the clarion call that you've given in your book?

TM: I think that what makes it confusing is when you go into these domains, the encounter is so emotionally powerful. The situation is so novel that the experient tends to assume that this emotional power is coming from the input. It's not. It's coming from the encounter with the input. It's like posing the question, "Can you make a stirring record of the Grand Canyon?" Yes, you can with a helicopter-mounted camera. But the emotion you have watching it, you bring to it. The psychedelic dimension is objective, but it's also so awesome and so different from what we know that it encourages and promotes and triggers awe in us. We bring something to it, which we can never image, or reduce to a verbal description or a piece of film. The thing itself is just more of reality, like the heart of the cell, or radar maps of the Venusian surface or the center of the atom.

RA: Do we need more reality? We've already got so much.

TM: We need more of this mental Logos world. It's a world that we've lost the connection with. These computer programs, psychedelic drugs, dynamic modeling schemes are the equivalent of probes, like Voyager. They're sent not to an alien planet, but to an alien phase—space of some sort, one that we need connection to.

Rupert Sheldrake: I agree. The problem is that the emotional intensity of a psychedelic experience is totally different from seeing a computer graphic display. It's possible to get something a bit like that just by shaking a kaleidoscope and looking into it. In these expensive novelty shops that dot California, you can find fancy, beautifully made kaleidoscopes. You look through them, and you can see a dazzling display of pattern and color, but within a few seconds you're just bored. Nobody ever really looks at them for very long. Somehow they lose meaning. It's no longer engaging.

I think the difference between representation of the state and being in the state itself is this sense of finding meaning, engagement and intensity. I for one, as a botanist, am very drawn to flowers. I love looking at flowers. Sometimes you can look at a whole garden full of flowers like here in Esalen, and it's quite meaningless. At other times you can look at a single flower for a long time, you can go into it. It's like a mandala. You enter into that realm, and it takes on incredible meaning, beauty and significance. The same with butterflies and many other natural creations. It seems to me the problem is how to enter into that engagement, intensity and sense of meaning, rather than the representation of the pattern itself. There are plenty of patterns around in the natural world.

RA: These are space/time patterns. Although we say the words *space/time pattern*, we have no language for individual space/time patterns. As experienced by us, there is a kind of a resonance between patterns that somehow makes a resonance with different patterns of neurotransmitters in the visual cortex. Some aspects are perceived and other aspects are not, remaining invisible to our perception.

You've been speaking of flowers in the garden, or the images in the kaleidoscope. These are static patterns, and we have an extensive verbal language for that. What I'm suggesting is an expansion of our visual/linguistic capability in the direction of a universal language for space/time pattern, such that we could truly speak of our experiences and give them names. At the mere drop of a word or a code, an I-75, Highway 1, Highway 0, we would transmit a clear image of space/time pattern along with whatever emotion we remember from the experience. If we can awaken these feelings in the mind of the listener, we can intellectualize, understand, reconnect and converse with the space/time pattern of the spiritual world.

Let's face it, we have the most extensive experience of this world through visual metaphors of, well, movies. We experience the Logos as movies. We don't experience it as words, although there are sounds, and there is sometimes writing on the wall like graffiti. Basically reality is an infinite field of consciousness, of vibration, of waves moving, of intelligence. When we travel in this realm, we go somewhere we've been before and we recognize it, and that excites in us memory, which is reinforced and extended, and upon this experience we base further experiment. We three have had our many experiences, which I have great faith, are similar, even universal experiences, and yet we are absolutely speechless in verbalizing them to each other. Words fail us.

TM: It seems that mind responds with an affinity for itself. If an expression is universal, then it has an affinity for the universal mind. What's interesting about the example of the kaleidoscope is that the kaleidoscope gets boring after a few minutes. If you analyze how it works, and take it apart, the base units in most kaleidoscopes are pieces of broken glass, pebbles, detritus, junk. Somehow splitting this into six sections with a mirror and putting it in heavy oil is supposed to bring you into the realm of something endlessly watchable and interesting. But it doesn't.

The brain machines being produced in Germany are the same way. All pattern seems to quickly lose its charm unless it's pattern that has been put through the sieve of the mind. We enjoy looking at the ruins and artifacts of vanished civilizations a lot more than random arrangements of natural objects. It seems to me what we're looking for when we say the MPP (Massively Parallel Processor) data on chaos is like a DMT trip, what we're saying is, "Here in this pattern is the footprint of meaning." It's as though an architect passed through. We're always looking for the betraying presence of an order that is more than an order of economy and pure function. We look for an aesthetic order, and when we find that, then we have this reciprocal sense of recognition and transcendence, and this is what the psychedelic experience provides in spades.

A critic of the psychedelic experience would object saying, "Of course it's made of mind. It's made of your mind." For the psychedelic voyager, the intuition is made of mind, but not made of my mind. Either there's an identity problem, or a real frontier of communication is being crossed. When we look for living pattern, or aesthetically satisfying order, what we really look for is a sign that mind has somehow touched the random processes of nature.

RS: The limiting factor seems to be neither the richness of display that we find in nature, nor the language that we communicate with, but rather the ability to go into something with intensity of vision. I don't think language is a limiting problem. For example, music can be written down in a language. I can read music, but for me it doesn't come to life from this language. I have to hear it for it to come to life. Presumably mathematical notation is a way of notating things in the mathematical landscape, which comes alive for mathematicians.

Take the realm of plants again. If you look at the incredible richness of botany, of flower forms, there is a language for this, used by botanists and florists, describing the species of plants in technical jargon. Even so, it doesn't mean that most botanists spend most of their time contemplating the beauty of flowers. They're rushing to the next committee meeting or getting their next paper ready for publication in a technical journal. Somehow there isn't much time to actually enter into these realms, even for people whose profession it is to be concerned with them. We're neither short of images nor of languages in many realms, but rather of the time, the space, and the inclination to enter.

RA: Music is a good metaphor. Let's just think of this for a minute. I don't propose that a mathematical model of a brain or a plant would be as wonderful as a brain or a plant. Life will not be replaced by language. Nevertheless, the evolution of music has been enormously facilitated by having a graphic language that to some extent recalls the actual musical experience. This is the role that I'm proposing for mathematics, not to replace the Earth or the heavenly realms, but to facilitate their understanding through an analog on the same level as musical staff notation, pertaining to the visual experience of space/time patterns.

What I'm suggesting is an increase in our encyclopedia of models, extending language, so that we can name, store, retrieve, and recreate not the experience itself, but the data, for the sake of communication. This is exactly what musical staff notation did for music. It pertains not only to the spiritual experience, but also to fundamental questions on the future of human society. Can we understand the space/time nature of the planet well enough, since it's so complex, to be sensitive enough to cooperate with it? If we can't even understand what we're seeing when we look, there's not much we can do to cooperate. Biogeography, for example, is a botanical field that could be revolutionized by a staff notation for space/time pattern.

RS: Surely what we're looking for is meaning in terms of significance. In terms of information, even patterns, we've got libraries full of informational models. Go into any bookshop, and you're overwhelmed by the quantity of stuff there. The idea of having even more models on the shelf somehow doesn't seem very exciting to me. What would be exciting would be to see some deep meaning in all of this. Maybe mathematics is one way to find the deep meaning in things. If so, I'm not quite sure how.

RA: The taxonomy of plants is not full of meaning, nevertheless a vocabulary has evolved so that when a word like *exfoliate* is put on a page, another botanist can read it and actually tell what kind of plant it is. A further development in the evolution of language is the generation of meaning. Meaning is not given in the data. We have to grok things. We have to struggle and evolve understanding by some hermeneutical process. People said when printing began, that it would be the end of memory, and when writing began, it would be the end of history.

TM: In both cases they were correct.

RA: Yes, when language began we lost our connection with the natural world.

TM: Maybe it was the kind of language.

RA: Spoken language.

TM: Language processed acoustically. It's not in the generation of it that you want to put your attention, but in the reception and decoding of it. When language became something acoustically processed, it became the willing servant of abstraction. Whereas language processed visually is here-and-now stuff of great density; acoustical language permits a level of abstraction that creates a higher inclusiveness, achieved by a necessary dropping out of detail.

RA: I'm glad to hear you say so, since it always sounds like you think the Logos itself is speech.

TM: Speech beheld.

RA: I'm astonished at the resistance I'm getting here to the idea of visual language. When I travel in France, may be riding in the train, I'm really bothered by all the gossip going around because I understand French. I realize that this couple is having trouble, and the train is not stopping in the station that I expected, and so on. When I travel in Japan, I don't understand anything, so it seems to me really very quiet there. I just don't hear anything. Where we have an oral language for certain phenomena, we then perceive it. It's like a moving van comes along and transports this stuff from the unconscious system to the conscious system, where we can deal with it.

These space/time patterns for which we have no visual language, are essentially unconscious to us. Therefore we can't interact with them, and this might be a fundamental reason that the planet is dying. Either we shouldn't have verbal language, or we should have verbal language and visual language as well. Verbal language is poorly adapted to space/time patterns. For example, we describe music with staff notation, a visual rather than verbal language. I think that our intellectual relationship to the sky and to the earth would be vastly improved by developing a larger closet of models for visual processing.

TM: I think you're right. I regard language as some kind of project that's uncompleted as we sit here. The whole world is held together by small mouth noises, and it's only barely held together by small mouth noises. If we could have a tighter network of communication, we would in a sense be a less diffuse species. Communication, or the lack of it, is what's shoving us toward the brink of possible planetary catastrophe.

If we buy into the idea that psychedelics are somehow showing us an evolutionary path yet to be followed, then it seems obvious this entails a further completion of the project of language. Maybe what all this technology is about is a more explicit condensation of the word. Modernity is characterized by an evermore explicit evocation of the image. We just have to go back 100 years, and the best anyone could do was to produce an albumin tint photograph. Now we have color lithography.

RA: High Definition TV.

TM: HDTV. Highspeed printing. Virtual reality. The worldwide web. It's as though language is becoming flesh. Meaning condensing into the visual realm would be a kind of telepathy compared to the kind of linguistic reality we're living in now.

RA: Glad to hear it.

RS: One final point I want to make. The model you are suggesting takes us further into the artificial manmade world of technology, and we've still got an incredible diversity in the natural world that hardly anyone's interested in anymore. There are herbaria collections, plants and butterfly collections, geological museums with rocks and crystals of every kind, and they're deserted. There's an incredible diversity of form in the natural world, and we are becoming more and more plugged into the entirely human world of technologies and man-made patterns. How does this relate to giving us a greater sense of connection with the bigger world?

RA: I believe that our connection to the natural world will be enormously enhanced by the new media, in spite of the fact that most people will relate to it as a new form of drug. I think that planetariums, for example, which are artificial models of the sky, brighter and simpler and easier to understand, can have an enormous potential to turn people on to the real sky, which is after all the ultimate source of our mind, our intellect, our mathematics and language. Although the construction of planetariums in big cities around the world is an expansion of the synthetic world at the expense of the natural one, the whole idea of them is to try to turn on a switch in some few people, making them aware of what was there all the time. I think a HyperCard stack with high-speed, high-quality color pictures and sound, giving all the beetles in the Amazon jungle, would enormously help me personally to understand what I'm seeing when I actually go there.

TM: I'd like to defend Ralph. I don't think that it's really a journey deeper into artificiality. Science has been dependent on instrumentality for a long, long time. The natural world that Ralph's program would reveal is the natural world of syntax. In other words, language would become a much more accessible object for study if it were visually explicit. And I expect that this is happening. It seems to me that we have reached a new frontier in the natural history of this most complex and least understood of all behaviors: language. While the instruments may be computers or high-speed imaging, and so forth, it's no different from using the Hubble telescope to tease data out of a very distant part of the universe, and then making it explicit. If we could understand language, we would understand something about our own place in nature that eludes us. It's clearly the most complex thing we do, and we're the most complex thing we know. The feedback from language is culture, the most anomalous phenomenon in the natural world.

RA: I want to end by saying this: Mathematics is part of the natural world. It's a landscape that can be explored, simply and directly, and with incredible pleasure, delight and advancement, just like the psychedelic Logos, or any other aspect of the world. The mathematical landscape does not belong to the human species. It belongs not even to the earth, but to the sky. It's part of the infinite universe we live in. Whatever microscopes, telescopes, kaleidoscopes, or computer graphic tools we can devise to enhance our vision of the mathematical universe is definitely advantageous. How this will fit into society, however, is a problem. We are in an evolutionary challenge from which the human species may not survive. I feel that part of our difficulty is our culture's rejection of mathematics. Mathematics is essentially the marriage of Father Sky and Mother Earth. I've given my life work to understand this relationship between the psychedelic and the mathematical vision. So I'll leave it there.

Science completely marginalizes human experience. We are told that we live on a typical planet around a typical star at the edge of a typical galaxy, and that we are animals of a complex type, easily identified with other typical forms. My notion is to take seriously the apparent vectoring in of universal intent on the human world and at the same time try to keep away from the pitfalls of religion. The ride to the end of history is going to be a white-knuckled experience. I offer this metaphor in the hope that it may make the trip to the transcendental object, glittering at the end of time, an easier ride.

CHAPTER 3

TIME

*T*erence McKenna: The subject for this trialogue is near and dear to my heart, you might even say it has my initials on it. I'm very interested in time, the largest frames into which phenomena can be fitted, and the various ways in which we can view our humanness when we change the way we look at time. What orthodoxy teaches about time is that for reasons impossible to conceive, the universe sprang from utter nothingness in a single moment. Notice that this idea is the limit test for credulity. If you can believe this, then you can believe anything. It's impossible to conceive of something more unlikely, yet this is where science begins its so-called rational tale of the unfolding of the phenomenal universe. It's almost as if science said, "Give me one free miracle, and from there the entire thing will proceed with a seamless, causal explanation."

There's an aspect to the phenomenal universe that impinges on anyone who undertakes to examine it, one that isn't given any weight whatsoever by science. When we look at the span of time that stretches from the big bang to the present moment, it's very clear that complexity has aggregated toward the nearer end of this process, the dimension in which we find ourselves. For example, the early universe was very hot, and only a kind of electron plasma could exist. By cooling, complexity appears, and each successive advance into complexity occurs much faster than the stage that precedes it.

But what I want to concentrate on is what I call the "short epochs." The first billion years of the life of the universe was an extraordinarily boring and empty period. Atomic systems were forming, and the simplest elements were aggregating into stars. This permitted fusion, the cooking out of heavier elements, and after a long period of time, the appearance of four-valent carbon, which permits a whole new set of properties to emerge, including ultimately, life. My terminology is largely drawn from Alfred North Whitehead, a great-unsung hero of British twentieth century philosophy. He had a notion of a progression of epochs leading toward what he called "concrescence." I've taken his notion of concrescence and attempted to construct a terminal cosmology that literally stands on its head the scientific explanation of the origin of the universe. I don't believe the universe is the push outward into substantial existence by primal explosion. I believe the universe is being pulled and shaped into an ever more complexified and concrescent entity that is in fact a transcendental attractor located in the future. It's transcendental in the sense of residing in a higher dimension than ordinary space, and in the feeling/tone sense in which we ordinarily use the term "transcendental."

This idea is basically Catholicism with the chrome stripped off. It restates Teilhard de Chardin's idea of the Omega Point, the *telos* attracting and drawing history into itself. What I'm interested to consider is that most delicate of all questions in prophetic systems of this sort: What is the role of humanity in all of this? Science evades this issue by setting us down somewhere between the big bang and the heat death of the universe, imagined millions of years in the future. Science completely marginalizes human experience. We are told that we live on a typical planet around a typical star at the edge of a typical galaxy, and that we are animals of a complex type, easily identified with other typical forms. My notion is to take seriously the apparent vectoring in of universal intent on the human world and at the same time try to keep away from the pitfalls of religion.

I think that history is the shockwave of eschatology. This is a concept we've not sufficiently entertained, but which we will be forced to entertain as the planetary crisis created by modernity builds toward some kind of climax. What I mean by saying history is the shockwave of eschatology is something like this: If this planet were a planet of hummingbirds, woodchucks, giraffes and grasslands, then Darwinian mechanics as modified by molecular biology would be sufficient to explain what's going on. The fly in the ointment of that simple schema is us. We represent some other order of existence. My notion is that out of the broad moving stream of animal evolution, a species was selected, or fell victim to—the terminology can vary—the influence of an attractor pulling in the direction of symbolic activity. This is what we've been involved in through chant, magic, theater, dance, poetry, religion, science, politics, and the cognitive pursuit of all kinds, occupying, for all practical purposes, less than 25,000 years—a blink of an eye on the cosmic scale. This is the shockwave that precedes eschatology. An analogy can be seen in the undisturbed surface of a pond. If the pond begins to churn, it indicates some protean form moving beneath the surface, about to make its presence visible. This is the appearance of history on the surface of nature, a churning anticipation of the emergence of the concrescence, or the transcendental object at the end of time. It's been anathema to discuss this in secular society, even as a part of "New Age" secularism, because it's always been the province of beastly priests and their hideously hierarchical and constipated religions. Decent people have tended to turn away from it.

In fact, this is some kind of primary intuition about our actual circumstance. The reason it's important is because we now are in a situation of planetary crisis, where you don't have to be an enthusiast for Whiteheadian metaphysics or psilocybin, or the more arcane metaphors of Terence McKenna, to realize that we are approaching our limits. It's inconceivable to speak of 500 years in the human future. History is a self-consuming process, and all we need do at this point is extrapolate any of a number of curves. Here are some of my favorites: The spread of epidemic, sexually transmitted diseases, the proliferation of thermonuclear weapons, the dissolution of atmospheric ozone, the rise in world population. When these curves are extrapolated, it's very clear that we've taken business as usual off the menu.

Rather than seeing this as a situation driven by the momentum of bad historical decisions, I'd prefer to believe that what we're witnessing is something like a birth; something that's built into the laws of physics. We are literally on a collision course with an object that we cannot precisely discern, lying just below the event horizon of rational apprehension; nevertheless, our cultural east is streaked with the blush of rosy dawn. What it portends, I think, is an end to our fall, to our sojourn in matter, and to our separateness. It lies now so close to us in historical time, by virtue of our having collapsed our options in three-dimensional space, that you need only close your eyes, have a dream, take a shamanic hallucinogen, practice yoga, and there you will see it. It's an attractor that's been working on the species for at least a million years. I maintain that it is actually a universal attractor, and we represent a concrescence of complexity that is truly transcendental.

James Joyce wrote in *Finnegan's Wake*, "If you want to be phoenix, come and be parked, up ne'ant prospector, you spout all your worth, and woof your wings, the end is nearer than you might wish to be congealed." I'm carrying this same notion, because I think that otherwise we're going to be victimized by an enormous pessimism arising out of the bankruptcy of science, positivism, and ordinary politics. The ride to the end of history is going to be a white-knuckled experience. I offer this metaphor in the hope that it may make the trip to the transcendental object, glittering at the end of time, an easier ride.

Rupert Sheldrake: Thank you!

Could you define *Eschaton*?

TM: Ah yes, let me fill in the footnotes. The Greek word *eschatos* refers to the last things, the final things. The *Eschaton* is a neutral way of naming what some call the Buddha Matraiya; some people call it the UFO intervention at the end of history, and some call it the Second Coming. It's the last thing, the *Eschaton*. What I think is happening is that all boundaries are dissolving—between men and women, between society and nature, and ultimately the boundaries between life and death. We are going truly beyond ambiguity, beyond syntax. We've been trapped in a kind of demonic simulacrum for 25,000 years, created out of language. Now the accelerating process of involuted connectedness characterizing this Whiteheadian progression of epochs toward the concrescence is in fact being fulfilled.

Ralph Abraham: This sounds a little more optimistic than I've heard you before. You've accepted the Big Bang fantasy of science, and then reflected it into a similar event coming in the near future, about which you're concerned with the "when." You haven't mentioned the date this time.

TM: I thought we could undertake a sort of generalized discussion of the assumptions that come out of this kind of thinking.

RA: For the first time I've heard you describe this forthcoming event as a birth. You interpret this optimistic event as an *Eschaton*. This is a myth made real, like the Christmas tree, where the events of history are kind of pasted on. As the tree shapes to a point at the top, you've drawn history around it, in an ascending spiral that ends at the point where they put the star. I think history can be wound on the form of this myth in a lot of different ways. You start with an assumption that's very symmetric and identical to the scientific myth of the birth of the universe.

This puts me in mind of the history of history, where the concept of time in different cultures suits different models, of which there are only a few. There's the bang to bang model, which you share with Teilhard de Chardin. There's the infinite linear progress model, which is pretty much discredited now by everyone. There's the reflection model, where a cycle is completed and then repeats from the beginning in a cycle of epochs that may be never ending. There's the Kurt Gödel model, in which time goes forward and encloses on itself by going around a torus and coming back. Many ancient societies shared this model, where every action we are doing today will be repeated again another day. These different models for history are essentially mythical structures; that is, no scientific evidence can be given to distinguish one from other. They start on the basis of belief.

Now that we have archeology and cultural history, we know there are different models of time, historically, and that they fit into certain patterns. If it's possible that what we do, think, or say affects the future, then it's important which historical model we choose, because the myth itself guides action, determines evolution, and influences to a degree the outcome. I don't see, though, even accepting the Christmas tree model, why the point with the star should be a birth or a death, or anything other than a simple cultural transformation, more or less presaged by a shockwave at the end of this epoch. Why couldn't it be just a simple social transformation like the Renaissance?

TM: Because the planet can't bring forth the birth of new societies. We've come to the end of our road in birthing new models of community. Wouldn't you agree that when we look back over the whole history of life as known to us, it appears to be some kind of strategy for the conquest of dimensionality? The earliest forms of life were fixed slimes of some sort. Then you get very early motility, but no sense organs, where organisms literally feel their way from one point of perception to another. Then comes sequestering of light-sensitive pigment upon the outer membrane, and the notion of a gradient between here and there appears. Then for a long, long time there's the coordination of backbones, skeletons, binocular vision and so forth. Then, with human beings some fundamental boundary is crossed, ending the conquest of terrestrial space, and beginning the conquest of time, first through memory and strategic triangulation of data out of memory, and then the invention of epigenetic coding, writing, and electronic databases. There's an ever more deep and thorough spreading out into time. In this *Eschatonic* transition that I'm talking about, the deployed world of three-dimensional space shrinks to the point where all points are cotangent. We literally enter hyperspace, and it's no longer a metaphorical hyperspace. What we're saying is, this transition from one dimension of existence to another is the continuation of a universal program of self-extension and transcendence that can be traced back to the earliest and most primitive kind of protoplasm.

RA: Isn't this a fancy way of saying we're running out of time?

TM: Yes. Time is speeding up. There isn't much left. Someone said time is God's way of keeping everything from happening all at once. My notion is that we are caught—the transcendental attractor is a kind of black hole, and we've fallen into its basin of attraction. Now we're circling ever faster, ever deeper, as we approach the singularity, called the *Eschaton*. All of this exceeds rational apprehension. It lies outside the framework of possible description. We're on a collision course with the unspeakable. Contrasted with other animal life, we've been selected out for a very peculiar metamorphosis via information and the conquest of dimensions to become something completely other: a new ontological order of being.

RA: It's too early to tell. Everything has accelerated. On the one hand, the population explosion, the destruction of the biosphere, the seriousness and irreversibility of all this is climaxing. Meanwhile, we have language, this 25,000, 60,000, or at most 100,000-year-old artifact. We've developed such things as agriculture and the urban revolution. We have automobiles and airplanes and computers hooking us up. We have all this increase in the complexity and fractal dimension of life, more or less to our benefit. We have, as it were, a race between two processes, both of which are growing faster exponentially. We don't know for sure which one is growing more. Furthermore, the possibility of a miracle can't be ruled out, due to the fact that we wouldn't even have gotten this far without a whole series of them.

It's a subtle matter, the way in which the myth of *Eschaton* can interweave in this race between the two accelerating processes. What do you think, Rupe?

RS: I agree with you, this is a cultural pattern. The Judeo-Christian tradition takes further tendencies already present in early civilizations. There's movement towards some end time, envisioned in apocalyptic prophecy. The last book of the Bible, the Apocalypse of St. John the Divine, speaks of things not unlike those that Terence speaks of. As Terence is well aware, the apocalyptic nature of his thinking is a transformation of a vision that appears in Christianity and in Jewish, Messianic, and apocalyptic literature. The question is, to what extent is the pattern of acceleration you see in our culture a product of the fact that our culture is based on this particular myth of history? To what extent do these visions reflect some true perception of a cosmic process, something far beyond history? That's not easy to decide, because there's a self-fulfilling prophecy built into these cultural patterns. We're now seeing these dreams coming true in many ways. They've led our culture to emphasize novelty, innovation, and change, always moving faster and faster. We've now spread this aspect of Judeo-Christian culture to the rest of the world, and the prophecy now seems pretty global.

For me, the big question regarding this prophetic vision is whether there's a real influence of something beyond humanity, beyond history. Terence thinks there is, namely the transcendental object, the attractor; or as Teilhard de Chardin put it, the Omega Point. If this is the case, how limited is it in its range of application? Are we talking, as Terence sometimes seems to do, about something just happening on Earth, or as Teilhard de Chardin talks of the noosphere around the Earth, and the growing emergence of consciousness? Or are we talking about the transformation of the entire universe? There's the same ambiguity in the New Testament, where St. Paul writes, "The whole creation groaneth and travaileth in pain until now" (Rom 8:22).

If we're just talking about this planet, these accelerating changes, graphs, and extrapolations look pretty plausible. If we're talking about the solar system or the galaxy, however, I don't think astronomers in the last few years or decades have suddenly noticed curves in their charts rushing off to some extreme point, where we can expect stars all over the galaxy to turn into supernovae. Nor can we expect planets all over the solar system to collapse, crumble, collide or otherwise undergo dramatic alteration. The history that we're preoccupied with here and now, human history and the effects of human activities, doesn't, as far as we know, seem to be mirrored in changes going on anywhere else in the solar system, the galaxy or the cosmos.

TM: It's a difficult question. If we extend the search for a universal crisis beyond the Earth, the only evidence that has been offered by anybody is some kind of problem between nuclear theory, which has been very well established for 40 years, and the neutrino output of the sun. Searching for pathology beyond the solar system in the cosmic environment is, I think, outside the present reach of our technical ability. I tend to think, though the time wave that I've elaborated can be extended back into the pre-biological domain, that this is a phenomenon of biology I'm talking about. This is just one small planet, and biology is a process of conquering dimensions. Once it starts the process, as a primal slime, it accelerates and it bootstraps itself to higher and higher levels at tighter and tighter turns of the spiral, until it essentially exhausts and abandons the planet, carrying itself into another dimension.

RS: But the whole point about biology is that the earliest forms of life, mainly plants, were related to the light of the sun. All life on Earth is dependent not on merely terrestrial events, but on our relation to the sun and the wider cosmic environment. Even carbon and the other chemical elements on which biological life depends is fallout from exploding stars. Biology on Earth is rooted in a much larger ecology. I don't think the evolution of life on Earth can be regarded as merely terrestrial, merely biological, in that sense. Every human culture has recognized the importance of celestial influences of one kind or another: the sun, the moon, the planets, the stars, the sky. Influences from outside the Earth are working on us all the time. The transcendental object may be located or channeled through the sun, other stars, planets, or constellations: something to do with the astronomical environment.

TM: If it's truly a higher-dimensional object, then it's in some sense everywhere in this universe, and all routes of evolutionary progress may lead into it, as a kind of universal hologram of time and space, a galactic community or intelligence perhaps. In other words, spores or viruses or bacterium probably percolate and permeate through the physical universe, and wherever they come upon a planetary environment in which they can work their magic, life takes hold. From then on it's a battle in which life attempts to modify and control the abiotic environment, keeping it at equilibrium sufficiently for the program of bios to be put into place. That program is to grow from the initial seed and return to the higher, hidden source of all, outside the pleroma of three-dimensional space. It's a Gnostic return, an idea of alchemical sublimation and rarefaction. I see the cosmos as a distillery for novelty and the transcendental object as the novelty of novelties. When we formally refine that, we discover something like a Liebnizian planet, a monad of some sort, a tiny thing that has everything enfolded within it. This takes us to another dimension, where all points in this universe have been collapsed and become co-tangents. It's an apotheosis. The Earth is giving birth to a hyperdimensional being.

RA: Just to shock you let me take a position much more pessimistic than yours. There have been several close calls lately, with comets. Some people, William Whiston for example, or Immanuel Velikovsky, felt that the beginning of our planet was a collision with a comet. It seems to me that it's quite likely we will get hit by a comet—and even pretty soon. Suppose that this happened. We'd have an extinction such as there was 65 million years back, when Jurassic Park vanished into the ocean. Then, this entire biological miracle, accelerating to its own schedule, with exponential condensation toward the concrescence of the *Eschaton*, and the shockwaves from the transcendental object at the end of time, would be rendered totally insignificant. We'd simply encounter a car crash on the highway of the solar system, totally independent of the progress of biology on the planet Earth.

TM: It's entirely possible. I didn't want to bring it up because it's so Halloween-like. The transcendental object at the end of time may be nothing more than a five-kilometer-wide carbonaceous asteroid, that in a single moment will send us all up to the gates of paradise.

RA: You're trying to destroy my argument by appropriating it!

TM: As I've said, the dissolving of boundaries eventually means the dissolving of the boundaries between life and death itself.

RA: If the *Eschaton* is a comet rapidly approaching New York City, why is it necessary to have this increase of complexity, the population explosion, the destruction of the ozone layer?

TM: In the million years preceding the impact that killed the dinosaurs, an enormous extinction was already underway, that we've not been able to figure out. It's as if the Earth knew what was coming. What I'm suggesting is that biology knows. Biology has a complete four-dimensional or five-dimensional map of the planet's history. The map says: "A comet's on the way; let's get these monkeys moving," leading to the production of sufficient complexity that when the event of impact occurs, it will be transcendent.

RA: An opportunity to proceed into another dimension.

TM: All of history is a curious relationship with this intuition that nobody wants to face, but that nobody can quite get rid of. We're sacrificing goats and we're doing this and we're doing that, because we have this very restless feeling that all is not well in three-dimensional space and time. History keeps bearing this out. Now it's upon us.

Jorge Luis Borges, the Argentine surrealist poet, had the interesting idea that a species could not enter hyperspace, whatever that means, until the last member of that species perished. What's happening is that vast numbers of souls are accumulating in another dimension, waiting for us to decently depart this moral coil so that the human family in a body can find itself at play in the fields of the lord.

RS: I want to think this through a bit further. We used to think that there might be this great transformation of humanity in a kind of collective near-death experience, except it would be an actual death experience, brought about by a nuclear cataclysm. Although the bombs are still there, that model's gone out of fashion for some reason. We're now more into ecological apocalypses. We've got all these models. Let's assume there's a sudden transformation, where all of humanity is taken up into the transcendental attractor. Leaving aside the details on the Earth, what effect does this have on the rest of the universe?

TM: I think it's not an answerable question, but it is in fact what we will then set out to understand. We are literally packing up and preparing to decamp from Newtonian space and time, for the high world of hyper-dimensional existence. We may find ourselves in the grand councils of the-who-knows-what, or we may find something entirely unsuspected.

I have talked before about shamanism anticipating the future. If you pursue these psychedelic shamanic plants, you inevitably arrive at an apocalyptic intuition. I think shamans have always seen the end, and that the human enterprise in three-dimensional space has always been finite. In the same way that ontogeny recapitulates phylogeny as we look into the past, it seems reasonable to assume that death, which we have spent a thousand years turning into a materialist vacuum, is in fact not what we think. There's an enormous mystery hovering over our existence that's only unraveled beyond the grave.

I would never in my life have thought that I would be pushed to this position. I spent the first half of my life getting away from this kind of thing. However, the evidence of the shamanic hallucinogens is in fact that shamans have always done what they do via ancestor magic and higher-dimensional perception, and that death is not what naive positivism in the last 300 years has attempted to say that it is. I realize it's incredible to suppose that here at the apex of materialist, positivist, scientific civilization, we're going to make an orthogonal turn into an understanding of what lies beyond the grave, but in fact, this is probably the paradigm-shattering world-condensing event that is bearing down on us.

RA: Conversion in progress.

RS: Given all that, I want to know whether this has happened anywhere else. If it can happen on our planet, perhaps it could change the entire conditions of dimensionality throughout the galaxy, or better, perhaps, the cosmos. If it's happened on planets elsewhere in the galaxy, what effect do you expect it to have had on us already?

TM: When you explore the adumbrations of the transcendental object, you see all this transhuman, alien data that's essentially what it has been in its past history. You see the imprint of all life finding its way back to some kind of source that's in a higher plane. That's why it has this alien presentation. It has maybe a thousand civilizations poured into it, or ten thousand, or fifty million. Who can know? The universe is already old.

RS: I still can't work out whether we're talking about some planetary violence that gets hold of civilization after civilization, or planet after planet, causing them to auto-destruct in a particular way, or whether we're talking about some cosmic process.

TM: It seems to me just the continuation of life's program of conquering whatever dimensions it hasn't yet conquered. Probably that process is endless. Life is a chemical strategy for the conquest of dimensionality. It carries out its program, come hell or high water.

RA: Just like striking a match: biology comes to a planet and the flame leaps up. Then pretty soon it burns out, due to exhaustion of resources and the arrival of the shockwave of the *Eschaton* for that particular planet. Biology is extinguished once again.

TM: This idea provides a way of imaging what's happening without falling into the dualism's that haunt either a reductionist view or an out-and-out, gung-ho, no questions asked, religious conversion. There are orthodox cosmologies that support my contention of the possibility of universal collapse. Hans Alfven, at the Swedish Academy of Sciences, who wrote *Worlds-Antiworlds: Antimatter in Cosmology*, has suggested that the universe is what's called a vacuum fluctuation. This is a situation in quantum mechanics where a group of particles and antiparticles spring into existence and then annihilate each other. Because parity is conserved by quantum physics. An interesting aspect of these vacuum fluctuations is that quantum theory sets no upper limit on their theoretical size, merely saying that the larger they are the more improbable they are. The universe itself could be a vacuum fluctuation of some 1068 particles, springing into being, allowed by quantum physics. These have separated into a higher-dimensional space, and are in fact eventually at some point in the future going to reconnect to conserve parity. Alfven says that in this kind of a higher-dimensional collision, all points in both systems would appear to an observer to become cotangent instantly. What that would mean is the material universe potentially could disappear in a single moment. All that would be left is light, because light doesn't have an antiparticle. No one knows what the physics of a universe made only of light would be like. I suggest to you that our many myths and intuitions that link light to the process of spiritual advancement, and talk about the generation of the light body and so forth, may anticipate something like this.

Even within the toolbox of ordinary quantum astrophysics, there are ways of putting together the syntactical bits together like tinkertoys to produce incredibly optimistic transcendental and psychedelic scenarios.

RA: There's no way to personally leap into the dimensions of hyperspace in the birth event of the *Eschaton*. Not in quantum physics. I suppose we're talking about a different kind of thing. What about the timetable, Terence? So far it seems like your idea is pretty similar to Teilhard de Chardin's, except he didn't give us a timetable.

TM: You mean when do I think it will occur?

RA: Yes.

TM: It's weird to talk about this because it rests on a formal argument where you have to look at a lot of historical data. What I did was I produced curves that I felt were reflective of the ebb and flow of novelty in time. By fitting these curves to historical data, I slowly refined down a prediction based on spiral closure, which makes it happen much faster than you would expect. I predict concrescence at the winter solstice of 2012 AD. After I had made that calculation, I discovered to my amazement, that the Mayan civilization had a very complex cyclical and recursive calendar, and it also indicated that same date. I think if you take strict objective data curves and then put in the fudge factor of the unexpected, it seems pretty reasonable to suppose that at least there is a nexus of prophetic intensity of some sort, causing a number of traditions for some reason to focus on the late months of 2012 AD.

When I attempted to understand objectively what could be going on, using computer simulations of the star fields, it turns out that the December 21, 2012 solstice occurs at a helical rising of the galaxy. Once every 26,000 years in the procession of the Great Year, there's a winter solstice sunrise that catches 23 degrees Sagittarius on the plane of the galactic ecliptic. What does that mean? Who knows? Certainly not me. In Hamlet's Mill, Giorgio de Santillana and Herthe von Dechend two very well-respected historians of science, suggest that for ancient peoples there were somehow galactic gates or way stations of some sort, through which souls had to transit to make their way back to their hidden home. I find this stuff a bit too mediumistic, but nevertheless, it is an objective fact that a rare solstitial conjunction that occurs once in 26,000 years will occur on the date I chose, and I did not know this at the time I chose it.

RA: Let's look at this. We have here the coincidence of three different things. One we could fairly describe as a novel and very interesting kind of mathematical extrapolation of historical data that culminates in a point. The other two things, the Mayan calendar and the astronomical conjunction are both periodic phenomena. The Mayan calendar repeats the cycle of 26,000 years, and the great conjunction recurs every 26,000 years. They can be expected to recur at least once more before the sun gives its last gasp, and biology becomes extinct.

If we weigh these things equally, your mathematical extrapolation isn't the same as the shamanic reportage of a hyperdimensional investigation. It's more like academic scholarship, with a huge database of history and this imaginative curve used to extrapolate data. This suggests that your extrapolation curve could actually be reversed so that you have a completely different model. It's not an ironclad extrapolation, and I think the case for this date actually being the Omega Point is weak. As far as the transition of all of us into the fifth dimension, I don't see a necessary case for it.

TM: What it comes down to is a very fine-tuned argument looking at a particular historical curve that's a damped oscillation. The curve of history actually does run down. It's not elegant to try to make it one cycle within a larger or extrapolated set of larger cycles. The built-in damping factor makes it pretty clear that it's a single cycle, with many cycles embedded within it, but on the highest level, actually having a beginning and an end.

RA: It seems to you radically implausible that there will be any future after this point.

TM: I've thought of many, many ways of expressing this that would make it less catastrophically radical. A very simple way that makes everybody feel a little better is to suppose that what happens on December 21, 2012, is that physicists who've been laboring for some time toward the technology of time travel, actually succeed. Suddenly the timewave is fulfilled, and yet the heavens do not fall, and angels don't appear to lift us into paradise. The reason history ends at that date is because after the invention of time travel the notion of a serial of events ceases to have any meaning. Everybody agrees history ended yesterday. We then experience life in a post-historical a-temporal bubble where you not only tell where you live, but when you live.

There are other alternatives. How about this one: On December 21, 2012 AD, I drop dead. Everyone says, "Well, how peculiar, it was only about him. He insisted and we were all swept along for 25 years in some bizarre mathematical machination, and the irony is he was able to foist it off on us."

It may not be planetesimal impact, or the oceans boiling, but I'm telling you, Ralph, there's something out there. I'll know it when I see it, and I'll expect you at my elbow.

I'm an unfortunate bearer of this message, because if you knew me, you would know that I'm actually not a very pleasant or nice person. Believe it or not I hate unanchored speculation! Yet I find myself in the predicament of leading the charge into the greatest unanchored speculation in the history of crackpot thinking. My method is very formal. It's very easy to predict the future, because who the hell can say you're wrong? It's a free-fire zone. Retrodiction, explaining or interpreting the past, on the other hand, is very difficult, because it's already happened. If you're wrong, everyone will know. What I've done is make a career of explaining the past with a wave that proceeds right past the present moment and into the future. My argument to the skeptics is that my wave has correctly interpreted any past moment that you can conceive of. Therefore, there's a certain intellectual obligation to at least take seriously the contention that it predicts the part of history that has not yet undergone the formality of actually occurring, as Whitehead might say.

RS: I've got one final question I want to ask you. Other people who tell us the end is at hand, as in placards reading "The End is at Hand, Prepare to Meet Thy Doom," suggest that this requires some kind of moral preparation on our part. Does yours come willy-nilly, no need to get ready for it in any particular way, or does it require some special preparation?

TM: This is a very difficult question. Much of what I was involved in many years ago was political activism, political struggle. Yet, when I go to my sources on this matter, they assure me that it's a done deal. Possibly one might spend one's time reassuring other people, but only if you felt like it. The walls are now so high, the creode, or matrix, so deep, the momentum so tremendous, that I really don't think anything could swerve or divert us from what we are being drawn into.

RS: I wasn't thinking in terms of more recycling and so on. I was thinking in terms of conscious, moral preparation.

TM: I think people should drive out and take a look at the *Eschaton* at the end of the road of history. What that means is psychedelic self-experimentation. I don't know of any other way to do it. If you drive out to the end of the road and you take a look at the *Eschaton* and kick the tires and so forth, then you will be able to come back here and take your place in this society and be a source of moral support and exemplary behavior for other people. I think that as we approach the *Eschaton* you will find that history is, as I said, a white-knuckle ride. There is an outlandish amount of vibration. It's going to look good, then bad, then worse, then good, then bad. If you haven't driven out to the end of the road and taken a look at what's waiting the next few years are going to drive you nuts, because the resonance of all past time is now in the close packing phase as the thing is squeezed down. The contradictions are rubbing up against each other. Boundaries are dissolving all around us. The Soviet Union, gone! Yugoslavia, gone! America as a great power, gone! Good taste, gone! This is going to happen faster and faster and faster. Governments are all managing a spreading wildfire of uncontrolled catastrophes, and trying to keep us in the dark about how bad things really are. It's good to go out and take a look and reassure yourself that the transcendental object is still there.

To put it simply, if you had the consciousness of a pigeon, you would not have a diminutive form of human consciousness. You would have a consciousness that we can barely conceive of. The consciousness of the pigeon is a continual awareness extending from birth to death

CHAPTER 4

HOW DO PIGEONS FIND THEIR WAY HOME?

Rupert Sheldrake: In my book *Seven Experiments That Could Change the World,* I focus on areas of research that have been neglected by orthodox institutional science because they don't fit into its present view of the world. As we have already discussed, this research can be done on very low budgets.

The experiment I propose with homing pigeons is one of the most expensive in the book but even so need cost no more than about $600. In spite of over a century of research, we really haven't a clue how homing pigeons find their way home. You can take a homing pigeon 500 miles from its loft and release it and if it's a good racing bird, it will be home that evening. Pigeon racing enthusiasts do this regularly. The birds are taken away from the homes in baskets on trains or on lorries. Then the baskets are opened, and the pigeons circle around and fly home. It's a very competitive sport. Pigeon fanciers win cups and cash prizes, and good racing birds can sell for as much as $5,000.

Pigeon homing is a phenomenon that everyone agrees is real. Moreover, many other species of birds and animals can home, including dogs and cats, and even cows. But no one knows how they do it. Charles Darwin was one of the firsts to put forward a theory. He proposed that they do it by remembering all the twists and turns of the outward journey. This theory was tested by putting pigeons in rotating drums, and driving them in sealed vehicles through devious routes to the point of release. They flew straight home. They could even do this if they were anesthetized for the duration of the journey. The birds could still fly straight home. So these experiments eliminate theory number one.

Another theory is that they do it by smell. This is not intrinsically very plausible, since, for example, pigeons released in Spain can home to their loft in England downwind from the point of release. There is no way that smells could blow from its loft in England to Spain against the wind, but the birds get home. Experimenters have blocked up pigeons' nostrils with wax, and they get home. They've severed their olfactory nerves, poor birds; they still get home. They've anesthetized their nasal mucosa with xylocaine or other local anesthetics, but they get home just the same. So smell cannot explain their homing abilities.

The next theory is that they do it by the sun, somehow calculating latitude and longitude from the sun's position. To do this they would need a very accurate internal clock. Well, pigeons can home on cloudy days, and they can also be trained to home at night. They don't have to see the sun, or even the stars. If they can see the sun, then they use it as a kind of rough compass, but it is not necessary for homing. You can shift their time sense by switching on lights early in the morning, and covering their loft before sunset. For example you can shift their sense of time by six hours. Now if you take such birds away from home and release them on a sunny day, they set off roughly 90 degrees from the homeward direction, using the sun as a compass. However, after a few miles they realize they're going the wrong way. They change course and go home.

Then there is the landmark theory. The use of landmarks is inherently unfeasible, because if you release the birds hundreds of miles from where they've been before, landmarks can't possibly explain their finding their home, although they undoubtedly use landmarks when they're close to home, in familiar territory. In any case, this theory has been tested to destruction, by equipping the pigeons with frosted glass contact lenses, which mean they can't see anything at all, more than a few feet away. Pigeons with frosted glass contact lenses can't fly normally, and indeed many refuse to fly at all. Those that will fly do so in a rather awkward way. Nevertheless, such birds can be released up to 100 miles away or more, and although some of them get picked off by hawks, others can get within a few hundred yards of the loft. They crash into trees or telegraph wires, or flop down onto the ground, showing that they need to see the loft in order to land on it. But the amazing thing is that they can get so close when they are effectively blinded. Sometimes they overfly the loft, and then within a mile or two, realize they've gone too far, turn around and come back.

This leaves only the magnetic theory. Until the 1970s, most scientists were very reluctant to consider this possibility, because magnetism sounded too like "animal magnetism," mesmerism, and a whole range of fringe subjects they didn't want to mess with. It also seemed unlikely that pigeons could detect a field as weak as the earth's. However, it has been shown that some migratory birds can indeed detect the earth's magnetic field; they do seem to have a kind of compass. However, even in principle, a compass sense cannot explain homing. If you had a magnetic compass in your pocket, and you were parachuted into a strange place, you'd know where north and south were, but you wouldn't know where home was. You would need a map as well as a compass, and you would need to know where you were on the map.

But perhaps the pigeons have an extraordinarily sensitive magnetic sense, by which they can measure the dip of the compass needle. A compass needle points straight down at the North Pole and is horizontal at the equator; the angle of dip depends on the latitude. So if pigeons not only have a compass but also can measure the dip of the needle, they might be able to work out their latitude. This could, in theory, enable them to know how far north or south they had been displaced. But if they are taken due east or west of their home, the angle of the field is exactly the same as at home, and pigeons can home equally well from all points of the compass.

In spite of these inherent theoretical difficulties, the magnetic theory has been taken seriously by many scientists, not because it is particularly convincing, but because they think there must be some mechanistic explanation, and this is all that's left. Nevertheless, this theory too has been refuted by experiment. To disrupt the magnetic sense, pigeons have been treated experimentally in two ways. Firstly, they've had magnets strapped to their wings or their heads, in order to disrupt any possible magnetic sense. Secondly, they've been degaussed by being put in extremely strong magnetic fields that will disrupt any magnetically sensitive parts within them. These demagnetized pigeons and pigeons with magnets strapped to them can still get home. (The first experiments of this kind in the late 1970s seemed to show that magnets could reduce their ability to home on cloudy days. However, these initial results turned out to be unrepeatable, and many experiments have now shown that pigeons can home even on cloudy days, when any possible magnetic sense is disrupted).

That's the current state of play. Every hypothesis has been tested, and tested to destruction. They've all failed. The one remaining that you occasionally hear is, "They can hear their home from hundreds of miles away, because of extremely sensitive hearing." Even this won't work, because pigeons that can't hear can still get home. All the theories have failed. Nobody has a clue how they do it, although this ignorance is often covered up by vague statements about "subtle combinations of sensory modalities," without giving any details as to what this might mean.

Pigeon homing is the tip of the iceberg. There are many other phenomena to do with migratory and homing behavior in animals which are unexplained, including the migration of cuckoos, Monarch butterflies, salmon, and so on. Human beings may also have a directional sense, probably best developed in nomadic people like Australian Aborigines, South African bushmen, and Polynesian navigators and least developed in modern urban people. In summary, pigeons, like many other animal species, seem to have navigational powers that are inexplicable in terms of known senses and physical forces.

The experiment that I'm proposing is very simple, and I can outline it briefly. The evidence suggests there is an unknown sense, force or power, connecting the pigeons to their home. I think of it as a kind of invisible elastic band, stretched when the birds are taken away from their homes, pulling them back and giving them a directional sense. I'm not bothering at the moment to theorize about the possible physical basis of this, whether it's part of existing physics, an extension of non-local quantum physics, or whether it requires a new kind of field. That question is open.

Using this simple model of an invisible connection, the experiment that I'm proposing is the converse of those done so far. The usual experiments involve taking the pigeons from the home and watching them return. By contrast, my experiment involves taking the home from the pigeons, using a mobile pigeon loft, which is essentially a shed mounted on a farm trailer.

I've actually done this experiment, first in Ireland and secondly in eastern England. So far, I haven't been able to carry it past the first training phase. I found, however, that it is possible to train pigeons to home to a mobile loft. They don't expect their home to move any more than we do, and the first time you take them out, you move their home just a hundred yards. When you release them they can see perfectly well that it's not where it was before. They go on for hours flying round the place where it was before, until they go into the loft in its new position. That's just how we'd behave if we went home found our house a hundred yards down the street. Most of us wouldn't just go straight in; we'd probably go round and round in circles, around the place where it was before, looking awfully puzzled. That's what pigeons do. If you keep doing this, after three or four times, they just get used to it, realizing they're nomads or gypsies now. After this kind of training, they can find their home up to two to three miles away within ten minutes. The only problem is that they are usually frightened of the unfamiliar surrounding and are reluctant to enter it.

During the First World War the British Army Pigeon Corps had 200 mobile lofts in converted London buses. There's still one army that uses mobile pigeon lofts, the Swiss army, and they are doing some fascinating research. Unfortunately some of it is classified, being a military secret.

To go forward with the experiment, it would be best to do it at sea, with the mobile loft on a ship. After training the birds, you move the mobile loft 50 miles downwind from the point of release, so they can't smell it. If the pigeons find it quite quickly, flying straight there, this would suggest there's an invisible connection between them and their home. The next question would be, is it between the loft itself, or the other pigeons? To test this you leave some of their nearest and dearest in the loft, or you take the nearest and dearest somewhere else, to seeing whether they find the nearest and dearest, or whether they find the physical structure of the loft.

How the experiment will turn out, I don't know. If there's a new power force or sense involved, what might it imply? What might it tell us? Where would we go from there? This is the question I want to raise with you.

Ralph Abraham: Let me ask you for a couple of details. When they race the pigeons and these home lofts are all in different cities, different streets, and so on, how does it work? Does the wife of the pigeon racer sit at home and when the mate comes, pull out the cellular telephone and call headquarters?

RS: The racing pigeon has a little ring on its leg for the race, with its number and the race number. When it enters the loft, the pigeon fancier captures the bird, takes this ring off, and using a sealed time clock issued by the local racing pigeon federation, stamps the ring with the time it comes home. When they send in these tags with the time stamps they calculate from the point of release, the straight-line distance to each loft, divide the distance by the time, and get the average speed.

RA: Do they account for difficulties and anomalous obstacles encountered along the way?

RS: No. If they're killed by a sparrow hawk, they don't win the race.

RA: Does the home loft that they're racing to contain family members?

RS: Yes.

RA: There's a whole bunch of pigeons in the loft, and only one or two of them are racing?

RS: There are several racing systems. The birds need a motive to go home fast. In the winter, they don't home very well. Races are usually held in the spring or the summer when they've got mates, eggs and young, so they have an incentive to get back to their family. One widely practiced method is called the jealousy system; dependent on the fact those pigeons are monogamous, forming pairs that last at least for a year. The pigeon owners wait until the birds have paired up, then they take away the bird that they're racing, and let another bird approach its mate. Then the racing bird is taken away. When released it returns home really fast.

RA: The stronger the motivation, the tighter the morphogenetic elastic band.

RS: Yes.

RA: Now that I'm getting the elastic band theory down I'm ready to risk speculating on the question. This is my fantasy.

First of all, accepting the premise that ordinary fields won't do as an explanation, let's assume it's a kind of ESP. I'm thinking of bats, which have been studied in rooms with wires strung through them. At night, the bat will fly around missing the wires and avoiding the wall, using sonar. Suppose, based on bats, that the brain and the mind are able to image the results of sonar experiments, in the same kind of image that the eyes form. In other words, instead of only hearing the sound and trying to compute where the echo's coming from, the bat actually sees the room with its ears, in the same kind of representation as the visual. Then if somebody suddenly turns the lights on, the bat wouldn't hesitate and fall to the ground because it has to switch from system A to system B. The visual representation of the room would exactly overlay the sonar image. Similarly, dolphins have this huge melon-shaped sensory organ that receives sonar waves. Both in the case of bats and dolphins, the visual/sonar representation is more three-dimensional than ours is. This would give them, in a way, a kind of a higher IQ. Dolphins and whales, which also use sonar, may sense almost the entire planet as a three-dimensional object, with its curvature and so on.

If there were a sixth sense that homing pigeons and monarch butterflies have, and maybe us to a degree, then I'd suppose it would work like that. Going back to our pigeons, after they're rotated, doped, transported 500 miles and released, with this sixth sense they would consult a very detailed three-dimensional road map of the entire planet. Then they would orient the holographic three-dimensional image with the visual world; rotating things around to get them aligned, and then to fly in the map. Things like smells, the sun, the magnetic field, are factors, and they'll act as a kind of label on the map.

This still doesn't explain how they get home. They would have to know where home is marked on the map. Given a sixth sense with a complete road map of the world as a three-dimensional object containing smells, trees, magnetic fields, the sun and the celestial polar constellations and so on, there must be some kind of beacon where home is supposed to be. Even in this sixth sense theory, that remains a mystery. The pull of some sort of morphogenetic rubber band is one idea, if there's an obstacle between pigeon and loft, there would have to be some way to find a way around it.

I think the rubber band theory is too simple. Considering jealousy and so on, the longer the rubber band is pulled, the tighter it gets, which is the opposite of most fields that we know, where the farther you get away from home, the weaker is the pull. I would think that the rubber band is more like a beacon that's a part of this whole field. Then the question is how is the physical information of a location, especially a recently moved location, inserted into the field. This would be the final mystery to fill in the picture.

Terence McKenna: It seems to me, if I can download this into language, that the problem is not with the pigeon, but with the experimenter. We know from studying quantum mechanics that things are not simply located in space and time. This error is what Whitehead called the fallacy of misplaced concreteness.

I've always felt that biology is a chemical strategy for amplifying quantum mechanical indeterminacy into macrophysical systems called living organisms. Living organisms somehow work their magic by opening a doorway to the quantum realm through which indeterminacy can come. I imagine that all of nature works like this, with the single exception of human beings, who have been poisoned by language. Language has inculcated in us the very strong illusion of an unknown future. In fact the future is not unknowable, if you can decondition yourself from the assumption of spatial concreteness.

The answer to how the pigeon finds its way home is that a portion of the pigeon's mind is already home and never left home. We, gazing at this, assume that pigeons, monarch butterflies, and so forth, are simpler systems than ourselves, when in fact, our assumption of the unknowability of the future creates a problem where there is no problem. It's only in the domain of language, and perhaps only the domain of certain languages, that this becomes a problem.

To put it simply, if you had the consciousness of a pigeon, you would not have a diminutive form of human consciousness. You would have a consciousness that we can barely conceive of. The consciousness of the pigeon is a continual awareness extending from birth to death and the particular moment in space and time in which an English-speaking person confronts a pigeon is, for the pigeon, not noticeably distinct from all the other serial moments of its life. The problem is in the way the question is asked, and in the way human beings interpret the data that is deployed in front of them. After all, in the animal world, the future is always rather like the past, because novelty tends to be suppressed. Most things that happen have happened before and will happen again. My expectation would be that what we're seeing when we confront these kinds of edge phenomena in biology is a set of phenomena which, when correctly interpreted, will bring the idea of quantum mechanical biology out from the realm of charge transfer, intracellular and subcellular activity, and into the domain of the whole organism. I'm not sure this is the solution, but it does cause the problem to disappear.

RA: Are you saying that the entire life history of the pigeon is more or less determined at the outset, including the trip away from the loft and the trip back?

TM: It never went anywhere. It's only when you've laid over this a three-dimensional grid imposed by language that there appears to be a problem. In other words, there's some kind of a totality involved, but we section and deny it and then come up with a dilemma.

RS: What about the pigeons that get picked off by sparrow hawks on the way home?

TM: They doubtless see that as well. The real question I'm raising is to what degree does language create the assumption of an unknown future? To what degree does it dampen a sense of the future that I imagine to be very highly evolved in the absence of language?

RS: It's hard for me to grasp. Do you mean that when a pigeon is released, part of its mind is still at home, in the future, and this in some sense helps it to get back to the loft?

TM: You and I have talked about this before. You've always implied that the morphogenetic fields drive, push from behind.

RS: No, I've always said they pulled from in front.

TM: Then they're attractors. I am partly saying that, and partly that the consciousness of the organism is distributed in time in a way that makes it capable of doing miracles from our point of view. From its own point of view, there's nothing unusual going on at all.

RA: You wouldn't be at all surprised if, as a matter of fact, the race was won by a clever pigeon that actually vanished at the point of release and simultaneously appeared back in the loft.

TM: You're seeing it as some kind of virtual tunneling, as an amplified quantum mechanical effect. Perhaps this is the solution to the spontaneous combustion mystery. We pay great lip service to the idea that quantum mechanics is very important for life. Well, the mechanical nature of things at a quantum physical level suggests that if life is an application of those processes, then our apparent entrapment in three-dimensional space with an unknown temporal dimension is almost, you would say, habitual, not intrinsic. This seems very reasonable to me.

RA: I think your idea is good. I like it. If consciousness extends over a certain span of time, even a few days, it would explain a lot of things in the pigeon world. I still think it's important to know whether the future is totally determined, or if the consciousness of the future includes several alternatives. In the case of several alternatives, sooner or later the pigeon is presented by a fork in the road and has to decide which way to go. I think we're still missing here some kind of mechanism for the pigeon to follow the stretched rubber band of its own consciousness, occupying an extended region of space and time, so that its ordinary physical body ends up back where its consciousness ends. How does it do it?

TM: An analogy would be when you run a cartoon or a film backwards, and there's a spectacle of wild confusion, but miraculously, everything manages to end up in the right place. It isn't that there really are choices for a pigeon when it comes into awareness, but that it comes into all the awareness it will ever have. It's like having your deathbed memories handed to you at the moment of birth. Essentially, for the pigeon, it's a kind of play. It knows what's going to happen, its life unfolds as anticipated, but it doesn't even know that it knows. The pigeon doesn't have the concept "anticipated." It's we who are observing that have that concept, and we alone are tormented by an anxiety of the unknowable future, an artifact of culture and language. Things like monarch butterflies, pigeon homing, and some of these other phenomena are clues to us that imputing our consciousness into nature creates problems in our understanding.

RA: That means that except for ignorance caused by the power of language, we would have the consciousness of a pigeon and therefore see our entire lifetime. According to this view, the baby pigeon chick, upon pecking out the shell, is waking from a dream, looking around and realizing that, "Oh damn, I'm the one that's going to have to race three years from now and they're going to put this other jerk in there with my mate."

TM: You use language to portray the state of mind of the pigeon. That immediately collapses its four-dimensional vector into three dimensions and it becomes no longer a pigeon, but a person talking like a pigeon.

RA: Is the pigeon then aware or unaware of its entire history from birth until death?

TM: It's aware, but it's not aware that it's a history.

RA: Experienced as one timeless moment.

TM: We could go further with this and say this explains our own curious relationship to the prophetic and anticipated. Instead of, like the pigeon, having a 95 percent clear view of the full spectrum of our existence, by opting into language we have perhaps a five percent view of the future. We're tormented by messiahs and prophecies, and we lean toward astrology and computer modeling and all of these advanced tools that give us a very weak and wavering map of the future which we pay great credence to and worry a great deal about. I'm suggesting that if we could step away from language that we'd fall into a timeless realm where darkness holds no threat and all things are seen with a kind of great leveling and all anxiety leaves the circuits. Perhaps this is what Zen masters do and teach.

I'm suggesting one more version of The Fall. From the fourth dimensional world of nature, complete in time, we fell into the limited world of language and an unclear future and hence into great anxiety and conundrums like how do the pigeons find their way home.

RA: This suggests that we should stop talking and writing books and just hum.

TM: I've always felt that. Rather like a pigeon.

RA: Is this a polite way of saying that Rupert's homing pigeon experiment is a total waste of time?

TM: I think all experiments as currently understood are futile, because all, including I assume the experiments in Rupert's book, make the assumption that time is unvarying, and I don't believe that time is unvarying. I didn't intend to open this up on a general frontal attack of the epistemic methods of modern science, but in fact the idea that time is invariant is entirely contradicted by our own experience and is merely an assumption science makes in order to do its business.

RA: I believe that we have a case here of multiple personality in action and now I'm going to undertake to prove it. You are now suffering from hay fever. Suppose that Rupert did an experiment with homeopathic medicine, and the outcome of it was that a flower power was discovered which absolutely and instantly cures hay fever. Would you then be interested in the result?

TM: Sure, but as a practical matter, I don't think we should confuse our ideologies with our sinuses. You see, I would like to redefine science as the study of phenomena so crude that the time in which they are imbedded is without consequence. I suppose ball bearings rolling down slopes fall into this category. The things which really interest us; love affairs, the fall of empires, the formation of political movements, happen on a different scale, and there's no theory for much of what happens in the human world. In the human world the invariance of time forces itself upon us, so we create categories of human knowledge outside of time, like psychology or advertising or political theory, that address the variable time that we experience. Then we hypothesize a theoretical kind of time, which is invariant, and that's where we do all the science that leads us into these incredibly alienating abstractions.

This goes back to Newton, who said time is pure duration. He visualized time as an absolutely featureless surface. Now take note that Plato's effort to describe nature with perfect mathematical solids was abandoned long ago, because nowhere do we meet perfect mathematical forms in nature. The only perfect mathematical form that has been retained in modern scientific theory is the utterly unsupported belief that time, no matter at what scale you magnify it, will be found to be utterly featureless. There is absolutely no reason to assume this is true, since all experiential evidence is to the contrary. The problem is, if we ever admit that time is a variable medium, a thousand years of scientific experiments will be swept away in an instant. It's simply a house of cards that's better left where it stands.

RS: This seems to go a little bit beyond the problem of pigeon homing.

TM: It addresses the problem of experiments as a notion.

RS: If we take what you are saying down to the level of pigeons again, it turns out to be an elaborate version of the rubber band theory; "the rubber filigree," or something like that. Let's say we perform the experiment of moving the loft; it could show us something that goes beyond anything contemporary science would expect. It might or might not fit with your all-time theory.

TM: It does fit.

RS: Nevertheless, here we have an experiment, crude though it is, which would show that the existing scientific model is very inadequate. The rubber band theory involves a kind of attraction to the home and in that sense involves a pull in time, so it does raise all these questions about the nature of time.

TM: Do you have a theory about how it works? I don't see how morphogenetic fields are particularly helpful here.

RS: Yes. I think the morphogenetic field would include both the pigeon and its loft. You can separate them by moving the loft or by moving the pigeon. Either way, they're part of a single system. The pigeon's world includes its loft, its home, its mate, and all the rest of it. When you move them, they're now separated parts of a single system, linked by a field. The pigeon is attracted within this field, back toward the home that functions as an attractor. This is where Ralph and I have a different view of attractors. The pigeon is pulled back toward the field, not needing a road map of the whole of Britain. A road map is irrelevant. It just feels a pull in a particular direction.

RA: It's like the angel theory; that when I come to a fork in the road, a guiding angel appears from behind a tree and tells me which way to go.

RS: Roughly speaking, it is. You just feel a pull in a particular direction. You don't even think about it. I think that's how the pigeon does it, subjectively. I don't think it necessarily needs to see the whole of its future from egg to grave. I think it feels a pull towards home by this kind of invisible rubber band, which is actually like a gradient within the field towards an attractor, which is its home. That's how you'd model it mathematically. You wouldn't have to bring in the whole of the rest of Britain and a road map. If it did, however, need a road map to the whole of Britain or Europe, we'd have to ask the question how would it get it? It might tune into the collective memory of all the other pigeons that have ever gone on homing races. If a pigeon could access the collective pigeon psyche, or the collective memory of other species, if all birds could link up to what all other birds could see; then they would indeed have access to a global map of the world. I think that's probably going further than we need in this rather limited case.

In the case of young cuckoos migrating in the autumn from Britain to South Africa, independent of the parents that they leave a month earlier, they must be tuning in at least to a kind of collective cuckoo memory that includes features of the landscape over which they fly. The rubber band theory wouldn't necessitate even that.

RA: There still seems to be a mathematical or cognitive problem, when the loft is moved. The dynamical system, which extends essentially over the whole of the planet, wherever the pigeon may be released, has to receive the feeling of which direction to go. The question arises, how does the attractor, the loft, extend its field and directional instructions all over the planet? I don't think that the idea of morphic resonance helps here, because in the case of the moving loft, no other pigeon has flown to it.

RS: I'm not talking about morphic resonance, I'm talking about the field itself. Morphic resonance is a memory. Say you have a pile of iron filings and a magnet. The filings are drawn toward the magnet and you see lines of force between them. When you move the magnet, you see an immediate response.

RA: The loft itself simply functions as a magnet in another field that is not an electromagnetic field—a sort of emotional field.

RS: When you move the loft, it's just like moving a magnet. The iron filings or whatever responds automatically. That's basically the model I'm suggesting.

RA: And the reason that I can't find my car in the parking garage is because I'm not emotionally attached to it and I've never been in love with it. I should get an Italian car.

RS: In the human realm it could apply to finding people. My wife Jill does an experiment in her workshop where people form pairs and they first find each other by humming with their eyes closed. After they've got that, they find their partner just by feeling where they are and heading in that direction. I've tried doing this experiment with our children on the assumption that with children this effect might be very strong, and it turned out one of them was extremely good at finding me. Then I discovered he was peeping.

Maybe bonds between pigeons and their homes are comparable to the bonds between people and other people. Indeed, they may be related to the kind of social bonds that hold society together. When we say the bonds between people, we may mean something more than a mere metaphor. Perhaps there is an actual connection. We have many examples from the human realm, as when a child falls ill miles away and its mother immediately starts worrying and rings up to find out what's happening. This may be another manifestation of the same kind of rubber band effect. It may be an aspect of social bonding. The motive of pigeons to go home is social, not merely geographical. If it hasn't got mates, it doesn't bother.

There are cases reported by naturalists that when packs of wolves go out hunting, a wolf may be injured, and stay behind in a kind of lair. The pack goes on and kills an animal, quite silently, no baying. Then the wounded wolf takes the shortest line from where it was to the place of the kill and joins the rest of the pack for its meal. The tracks show that it goes in a straight line without following scents, because it can do this when the wind is blowing the wrong way. This kind of social bond and linkage may be fundamental.

RA: There's a kind of agreement here that there is a sixth sense that's a field phenomenon, like the quantum field. It's a social field, involved with the flocking of birds, the schooling of fish, and with herds of animals and packs of wolves. To answer the question you posed when you started us off; what would this teach us, or mean to us in terms of our future? It could be that humans are somehow divorced from the significance of this field, so whenever their guardian angel speaks, they always do the opposite. If we want to understand the population explosion, the demise of the planet, all these wars, the manifestation of hatred and sources of evil, a candidate for the disharmony in the human species would be its disconnection with this field. Here's where Terence's idea comes in, that somehow to submit to language is to lose our connection with the field. We've all done experiments in not speaking, for example meditation and dreaming, where the antitheses of language have an opportunity to come forward and reconnect us to this field. For people like Americans, who watch television seven hours a day, there may somehow not be enough time away from language.

TM: Notice that most prophetic episodes are dreams. This supports my point, that we've lost connection with a kind of fourth-dimensional perception that for the rest of nature is absolutely a given.

RS: Why do you think it's a given in the rest of nature?

TM: Because there are many, many cases of this kind of thing. Animals that are put in the pound by the owners who are moving, and then the owners move seven hundred miles and the animal escapes from the pound and it doesn't return to the ancestral home; it returns to the new apartment in a different city. The monarch butterflies, the homing pigeons, a whole host of mysterious phenomena become utterly transparent and trivial if you simply hypothesize that for them, the future doesn't have this occluded character that it has for us as a result of our acquiescence in language behavior.

RS: It's not just a problem in time, it's a problem in space.

TM: They see themselves at every point in their life, not just the high or low points.

RA: They're a minute ahead of where they are, so they just go that way.

TM: In other words they can always see their goal from where they are. They navigate through time in the same way that we navigate through space. I mean, if you were a two-dimensional creature, the things that we do, navigating in three-dimensional space, would be absolutely mysterious and generate all kinds of metaphysical speculation and hypotheses. Why should nature imprison itself within a temporal domain?

Clearly, for us it's an artifact of language. We talk about future tenses, past tenses that aren't descriptive of the future and the past; they create it. That's why I put in the possible exception of human languages where this is not happening and therefore they are much closer to animal perception. The "mysterious" behavior of Australian aborigines, or the Hopi. These people seem capable of things that to us are like magic, but the magic is all done by knowing what's going to happen. If they simply imbibe the animal's understanding, then to them it's trivial. This is the most elegant explanation, not requiring new, undetected fields, or any of these other somewhat cobbled-together mechanisms.

RS: Just another dimension.

TM: We know it's there. There's no debate about that. I've always noticed that all the magic done by shamans in aboriginal society, especially the ones that are using psychoactive plants, suddenly becomes not so mysterious if you simply assume that, by perturbing the ordinary brain states and ordinary language states, they let in this hyper-dimensional understanding. Look at what shamans do; they predict weather and they tell the tribe where the game has gone. Both require knowledge of the future. They rarely lose a patient, meaning they know who's going to make it and who isn't, so they can refuse all cases destined to be fatal. All these examples of shamanic magic can easily be explained by the simple assumption that they can to some degree perceive the future. Animals operate from this place to begin with. What is the shaman's strategy for attaining his special knowledge? He becomes like an animal, he is master of animals, he dresses in skins, he growls.

RA: He talks to pigeons.

TM: He talks to the animals, perturbing his brain state with ordeals or drugs or other techniques. The very close association of the shaman to the animal mind suggests that it's the clue to entering this a-temporal or fourth dimensional perceptual sphere.

RS: In the Christian tradition a principal symbol of the holy spirit—that which gives inspired prophecy, shamanic-type gifts of healing, and intuitions of various kinds—is the pigeon. The first Biblical story of the pigeon is in the story of Noah's ark, where the pigeon was sent off and came back with the olive twig. Right from the beginning the pigeon is a messenger who can find out things in distant places and return, bringing back the information.

*Even if we collide into this wall of history here on Earth, I find it
quite incredible that the rest of the solar system is just going to shut
up shop and go out of business, let alone the galaxy, let alone the
clusters of galaxies.*

*The historical record is compatible with the idea of an upcoming,
amazing, difficult, and creative social transformation in our immediate future.*

CHAPTER 5

BETWEEN THE APOCALYPSE AND UTOPIANISM

Ralph Abraham: Our project this morning is to try to
see ourselves as a trinity, and to experiment with the
idea of connecting with such traditions as are perceived by
cultural historians.

There are two particular themes that I want to describe, as
two possibilities for understanding ourselves in the historical
tradition, and they are utopianism and millenarianism. As
understood by cultural historians, utopianism is one of the
major currents of the European mind, and not an old one. The
concept of the ideal city in the ancient world, most especially
the ideal city of Plato's Republic, could casually be called a
utopian fantasy, although Plato tried to actually realize it in
the political organization of a particular city, and ended up in
jail. According to historians, utopianism begins on a particular day less than 500 years ago. That was the day of publication of Thomas Moore's book *Utopia* in 1516. This word
utopia is a translation into Latin of the Greek, *utopos*, mean-

ing nowhere. Its initial chief characteristic is that it was acknowledged to be nowhere. This was a dream not to be made real. It was fiction, having characters and plot and story, presenting various themes of ideal achievement for our culture.

After 1516 this book sold well, and had lots of imitators. There was a huge genre, a body of fictional works, which became the foundation of a utopian trend. Eventually this branched into nonfiction. The idea began to materialize in actual communities that tried to live up to the utopian ideals of some novel or nonfiction work. Riane Eisler's book *The Chalice and the Blade* is a perfect example of the nonfiction utopian work. Frank and Francie Manuel produced a book that looks back on the history of Utopianism since 1516. In this 900-page work they catalogued in order of appearance all the authors, works, and communities that started and then failed. The last chapter in the book is entitled "Twilight of Utopia." They saw the trend ending after 500 years, probably under the influence of our experience in the 1960s, when the hippies of California, Paris, Amsterdam, and other places tried once again to materialize a new utopian ideal in actual practice, even striving for a planetary society based on ideal lines. This attempt completely and totally failed, leading the Manuels to conclude that the utopian literary current had finally dried up and ended.

Nonetheless, since 1979 and the publication of the Manuel book, there have been surges of renewal in the literature. I've mentioned Riane Eisler's book, published in 1987. Another nonfiction work of this type is Rupert's book *The Rebirth of Nature*, first published in 1990. Then there's Terence's book *Food of the Gods*, 1992. I think certainly, if Mr. and Mrs. Manuel wrote a revised edition of their book, they would definitely include these authors in their list. My book, *Chaos, Gaia, Eros* could be considered a kind of chaos utopia. Rupert's book is a scientific utopia, Terence's a psychedelic utopia, and Riane Eisler's a partnership political utopia.

Paul Tillich, writing about this trend in 1951, pointed out the Trinitarian aspect of the utopian genre, harking back to the trinity of the prehistoric Goddesses, manifest in Christianity as the Holy Trinity—the Father, the Son and the Holy Spirit. He said that this particular Trinitarian utopian model was presented long before Thomas Moore in 1516, in the works of Joachim di Fiore in the 12th century.

Let me just read a few words of Tillich's understanding of the Trinitarian structure of the utopian genre, as I think this will help us to see ourselves in history:

> *The overwhelming majority of these utopias show a triadic movement. The original actualization, namely actualization of the essence, and then a falling away from this original actualization, namely the present condition. And third, the restoration, as an expectation that what has fallen away from its primordial condition is to be recovered. One of the distinguishing characteristics of this triadic movement is the consciousness on the part of those who use this symbolism, almost without exception, it is important that the lowest point of the falling away has been reached in their time, in the moment in which they themselves live. It is always the last period that gives birth to utopia. Illustrative of this and perhaps also the best formula that has been given for it is Joachim di Fiore's idea that we live in the age of consummate*

sinfulness. Also illustrative is Augustine's idea that the world empires that have come to an end were the last ones—the Great Roman empire, which he as a Roman loved—and that their sole successor is to be the kingdom of God, which is in some measure actualized in the church. But the final actualization will take place only after the close of history. This same idea is found in India, where it is always the last period in which the theologian, speaking of a succession of ages, finds himself. It's found in Greece, where the stoics speak about the Iron Age as the last and most wicked. It's in Marxism, where the class struggle running through the whole of history reaches a point where revolutionary changes become inevitable. In the fascistic ideologies, decadence reaches its final stage when counter movement must set in. All of these instances show that the triadic progression is centered on the moment in which the reversal is immediately eminent. This is characteristic of all utopian thought. (Paul Tillich, *Political Expectations*, p.134)

The other line of thinking we must address is millenarianism, which has roots in the Jewish idea of the Messiah; that there will be a coming of God on earth to rescue humanity from a fatal impasse. In the Christian tradition this evolved into the Apocalypse, described in the New Testament, where there would be a third coming of Christ in a transformational period lasting a thousand years. The idea of the millennium rises not only from the year 1000 or the year 2000, but also the idea of a special period of 1000 years that's transitional to our final salvation. Salvation is an important aspect of the millennial idea.

The millennial tradition actually begins after the year 1000, when many people were disappointed that the Messiah didn't arrive. Terence has referred to this three-year period, centered on the year 999, when everything came to a halt. After that time is the beginning of a new millennial hope, the growth of an extensive literature, and an extensive actualization in popular movements. These are always characterized by a prophet, the charismatic leader of a group of people, sometimes very extensive.

There is magisterial work on this movement by Norman Cohn, published in the 1950s, and revised after new discoveries in 1971: *The Pursuit of the Millennium.* This book is an incredible catalog of prophet after prophet, movement after movement, from the beginning, to the middle, to the end, including literature, analysis, and descriptions of all these movements. Like the utopian movement, this is an artifact of the European mind. It takes place primarily within the context of Christianity, these millenarian groups being without exception heretical, departing from one or another dogmatic aspect of the organized church. Outside of this Christian heretical tendency, they tried to organize communities that epitomized a certain communitarian ideal. Almost invariably they included sexual freedom in reaction to the idea of sin and sexual repression in the Christian tradition.

In Norman Cohn's revised edition there's an extensive appendix, which is a translation of virtually all of the extant literature of one particular group, which in the seventeenth century coincided with the rise of science in England. They were very popular in England, and were called the Ranters.

Reading about this group in particular brought up certain similarities with our experience in the 1960s, as well as the contemporary movement in which the prophet obviously is Terence.

The utopian structure is triadic. What we had before was good, what we have now is the deepest depression that will ever be seen in human history, and tomorrow the virtues of yesterday will be restored, together with new enhancements, or something that will be even better.

On the other hand, millenarians are dominated by the apocalyptic idea that human history will end at a certain moment with the *Eschaton*, culminating in some kind of final moment. Certainly two of the most outstanding exponents of this tendency today are Terence and Jose Arguelles, who agree not only on the *Eschaton*, but also on the date—the year 2012—having arrived at this time schedule following completely different approaches.

Between these two tendencies of the European mind, the Utopian and the Millenarian, there is a certain overlap as well as important differences. Somewhere in the neighborhood of this overlap I think we can see our own trinity in our ten-year history of doing what we're doing now. If this isn't too egoistic, considering ourselves in the light of these historical trends, at least we can say that these trends have influenced us, perhaps unconsciously, in coming to the positions that we've taken. In case this is so we might want to consider the outcome of other people who were under the influence of these traditions, as they unconsciously responded to these deep runnels in the morphic field of our culture. Here is the context for our self-reflection.

Rupert Sheldrake: This model is very illuminating. It clarifies a lot of things. I can see in myself both tendencies at work. The utopian tendency is something that's clearly expressed, for example, in socialism. I spent many years as a socialist, believing that there was this primal state of humanity living in brotherhood, followed by the alienation caused by serfdom, the feudal system, the rise of capitalism, the industrial state, imperialism, and so on, following a Marxist analysis. Then the capitalist order is overthrown and one eventually returns to a more primitive, non-alienated state of people living in communities, sharing their goods, and the state withers away. This is the Marxist utopian model, with a millenarian aspect as the revolution ushers in a new age.

I was also influenced by scientific utopianism, having been educated as a scientist. The primary scientific utopia is Sir Francis Bacon's book *New Atlantis*, published in 1624. In it he offers the vision of an entirely new order in the world. He portrays a Christian utopia with a scientific priesthood based in a place called Salomon's House, which is a college that rules an island kingdom. Someone is shipwrecked on the island and they find themselves in this ideal society. Everything is rationally ordered, and research is officially organized by the priesthood of Salomon's House: they have gardens where they breed plants, they keep animals to study in vivisection experiments, they have wave machines so they can study how to make dams and harbors properly, and they study artificial tides and storms on a small scale through models. They try to develop a universal language. Jonathan Swift satirized this in the third book of Gulliver's Travels, *Voyage to Laputa*, where there's a crazy academy whose members are engaged in preposterous projects, like making sunbeams out of cucumbers.

Anyway, scientific utopianism got built into the idea of technological and scientific progress, which was going to liberate mankind from the bondage of poverty, disease, and slavery to the elements of nature. In fact, it gave rise to the ideology of the modern world: economic development through science and technology.

Then there's the liberal political utopianism of socialists and liberals who have the idea that you bring about utopia not just through science and technology, but through economic and political reform. I believed all this for a long time, and I think most of us still do, because it's so deeply ingrained in our culture.

Then there's the New Age movement, which believes there'll be a new utopian age brought about through the rediscovery of ancient religious traditions, through the development of human potentials, and through holistic, harmonious ways of doing things. This is another kind of utopianism that has influenced me.

I think Ralph's right in saying that my own book *The Rebirth of Nature* is an example of the utopian tradition. The essence of my argument is that in the past people treated nature as alive, and a recognition of the sacredness of nature gave a better way of relating to it than our alienated, mechanistic way of treating nature as a bunch of raw materials to exploit for profit. Restoration of this sense of the life of nature could lead to a new kind of post-mechanistic culture in which human beings would be the mediator of the marriage of heaven and Earth, bringing human society into right relationship with both.

As for Terence, half of his thinking is utopian, the other half millenarian. The utopian side is the psychedelic revival, with its belief in an ancient society where people had a wonderful time living harmoniously on the Earth, with tremendous visions thanks to psychedelic plants, particularly mushrooms. Then it all went wrong. The climate changed, the Earth dried up, the psychedelic visions became less and less frequent, and a poor substitute took over, namely alcohol. One then plumbs the depths represented by modern society. But the original harmony can be restored by the mass consumption of mushrooms, the smoking of DMT, and other psychedelic activities. Thus dawns the psychedelic utopia.

Ralph's version is a mathematical utopia, where the great regulative, eternal structures of the mathematical landscape, the fundamental principles reflected in all nature, heavenly and terrestrial, become visible. Not only visible to the high priests of mathematics, but potentially to everyone through the medium of computer modeling. There's a kind of democratization of gnosis that direct knowledge of fundamentals, which mathematics has had as its guiding light through the centuries and the millennia. This Gnostic seeing behind the scenes becomes commonly available, not only through psychedelic visions, but through computer models which can be shared and entered into by many people.

When we consider what would happen if the millennium were postponed, if it didn't all happen in 2012, we are forced out of the field of millenarianism into the field of utopianism. Millenarians usually have the end conveniently close—not too close, but close enough so that it could be in our lifetime—2012 is a perfect date from that point of view. According to the millenarian scenario, and according to the Jewish and Christian apocalyptic books, most notably the Revelation of St. John the Divine, with which the Bible ends, the end of history involves appalling plagues, earthquakes, eruptions, and other disasters. Of course it's only too easy to see all these things coming to bear on our society, leading toward inevitable collapse and catastrophe. The only way out is total, miraculous transformation, the coming of the Messiah, the descent of angelic powers, or, in one of Terence's versions—he has many ways of imagining this end of history—some kind of collective DMT trip. The apocalypse amounts to a near-death and rebirth experience where we will pass through an appalling time of disturbance, and then emerge into a new realm of being. The apocalyptic tradition doesn't try to stop things getting worse; it regards this as inevitable. This is the conflict we all find ourselves in. We find ourselves becalmed in the area between the apocalypse and utopianism.

There's hardly anyone who's into the old-style socialist utopianism anymore. And who believes the world will be saved by more science and technology run by technocrats? The concept of enlightened transnational government, a vision underlying the United Nations or the European Union, still has some vigor and is still important, but I don't meet many people who are wildly enthusiastic about either as the solution to all our ills. These utopian visions that guided so much of humanistic and socialistic thinking in the twentieth century have put their trust in rational reform, education, science, technology and world government. The Rio conference on the Environment was an attempt to bring this approach to bear on problems such as global warming and environmental degradation. The results have not been impressive.

I'd like to ask you, Terence, how you see these two strands in your own thinking. On the one hand the archaic revival is psychedelic utopianism. On the other hand the time wave, ending in 2012, is millenarian. Since you represent both strands so eloquently, I'd like to know how you see them connecting or linking together.

Terence Mckenna: If we restrict ourselves to the realm of the rational, we only have two choices—utopia or more history. More history is beginning to look less and less likely. At the beginning of James Joyce's *Ulysses*, Stephen Dedalus says, "History is the nightmare from which I am trying to awaken." I feel this way. I can't imagine a thousand more years of human history—more wars, more discoveries, more topless photos of Fergie, more and more and more endlessly to no meaning. On the other hand, efforts to build utopia have become fiercer and more horrifying. In the twentieth century there were three serious efforts to build utopias: the American, the Nazi, and the Soviet. All have ended very badly, I think. The National Socialist utopia ended in the Second World War in an utter discrediting of fantasy fascism. The Soviet Union dissolved in disarray. The American story is in the act of unraveling at this moment. This leaves us to face the most unlikely of all scenarios, the millenarian, which is an irrational choice. The rational path is to fashion out of human plans, dreams and institutions some more humane order. That's the hope of utopianism.

I believe in the millennium, but I also think it's politically a disempowering idea. I see Christian fundamentalists running around who also believe in the millennium, and they're the major anti-progressive force in the most advanced societies.

How should we react to this dilemma? I think it's worth looking slightly afield for a moment. What we're really talking about here are origins and endpoints, and so far we've been looking at endpoints. What about origins? The dominant and virtually unchallenged myth of our origin is either God created us in seven days along with all the rest of creation, or the universe was born out of nothingness in a single moment for no reason. These are the two choices on the menu. Neither is terribly compelling to rationalists, I dare say. The scientific explanation however we may think of it in terms of its veracity—that the universe sprang from nothing in a single instant—is the limit case for credulity. If you can believe that, you can believe anything! Sit down and try and think of something more improbable than that contention. Science opens up with the one-two punch, saying, "Put that in front of them, and if they can swallow it, then hydrogen bonding, gene segregation, whatever, will follow hard apace." The hard swallow comes first.

Many creation theories require a singularity. That means that in order to kick-start the intellectual engine, you have to go outside the system. You get one free hypothesis, and once you've used that up, your system has to run very smoothly clear down to the end. Science uses up its one free hypothesis with the Big Bang, saying in effect, "Give me the first ten to twelve nanoseconds, and if I can do smoke and mirrors in that time frame, the rest will proceed in quite an orderly fashion." I think that if you get one free singularity in your model building, a more likely place to put it would be not in a featureless, dimensionless, processless super-vacuum at the beginning, but in a domain of many temperature regimes, many forms of energy, many languages, many chemical systems, many different levels of energy exchange, late in the life of the universe. What you have then is a picture not of a process being pushed by causality toward some heat death billions of years in the future, but one of a universe that is flowing naturally toward ever greater complexity, at the end. Organization transcends itself, produces more complex organization which transcends itself, which produces more complex organization, and conceivably, out of a process of avalanching complexity you might actually get a singularity of some sort. This singularity would have the character of an attractor. I grant you that this model is irrational, but our little discussion of the birth of the universe should convince you that it's ALL irrational. Irrationality doesn't get you tossed out of the game. It's the name of the game.

Being hopefully a sane person, my own inner dialogue goes back and forth between the reasonable desire to preserve rationality and hence channel energy toward utopian hope, and thoughts about the end of time. After all, we have the money, scientific knowledge, communication systems and so forth, to solve any of our problems—feeding the hungry, curing disease, halting the destruction of the environment. The problem is that we cannot change our minds as quickly as we can redesign harbors, flatten mountains, cut rainforests, dam rivers. Because I see this, and because I see it from a psychedelic point of view, and because I don't want to abandon myself to despair, I see then this transcendental object at the end of time. This is not part of the utopian schema. It is part of the millenarian revelation. It's a very persistent idea, and in all times and all places, this highly unlikely concept has been kept alive.

I think that we are blinding ourselves to the intentionality present in our world. I think you have to be carrying a lot of unusual intellectual baggage to not see the last thousand years as moving toward a maximizing of some set of goals. It's not the triumphal march into God's kingdom envisioned by Christianity, but neither is it the trendless fluctuation that is taught in the academy. If you go to a university and ask them, "What is history?" they will tell you it's a trendlessly fluctuating process. What they mean is it isn't going anywhere. Now that's interesting. If history is a trendlessly fluctuating process, then it is the only such process ever observed anywhere. Processes are not trendless; this is what dynamics has secured. Processes always occur under the aegis of some set of parameters that are being maximized. If a desert is drying out, then water vapor levels are dropping. What's being maximized is dryness. To think of history—the very process in which mind is embedded and through which it expresses itself—as trendless is an existential absurdity.

Plato said that if gods did not exist, human beings would create them. We are creating God. Our cultural machinery, our dreams of integration and balance, our care for each other and for the world—these are god-like aspirations. We aspire to be God when we talk about becoming the caretakers of the world. We don't want to be Adam and Eve chewing on the fruit in the garden. We want to be the gardener. The power that we have in our possession means we will realize these dreams. If there is not a real millennium with a real *Eschaton*, then there will be a virtual *Eschaton*, created with such care and fine attention to detail that it becomes an alternative reality of some sort.

If one were saying this will happen in a thousand years, or in 500 years, it would just be interesting table talk. But the rates of closure, the speed of acceleration toward the Omega Point, are exponential. We cannot imagine 2012 by looking backward 20 years and then saying we have that much more time to go through before we reach this moment. Cocktail party habitués bore each other by observing, "Have you noticed that time is speeding up?" Time itself is moving faster, and we are compressing more events into it. I would like to take that seriously. Time is speeding up. Not human time, but the time of physics. We can imagine ourselves colliding with an asteroid or being battered by earthquakes or something like that, but what we cannot conceive of is that we are on a collision course with a hyperdimensional object of some sort.

People always object to the millenarian intuition with, "Well, you say a transcendental object is coming parallel or tangential to history—don't you find it a little odd that out of billions of years, it's going to occur in your lifetime? How convenient." This is not an objection at all; it's an argument in favor of my position. You see history is the trumpet of judgment. A million years ago there were only animals and plants and rivers and glaciers on this planet. Human history is the annunciation of the *Eschaton*. When you open a door, first there's a crack of light that streams into the darkness. That's human history. We have cracked the door. That moment only lasts about 25,000 years, creating an order in nature never before seen, represented by a technological, language. When you push the door open, you see that history is the shock wave that precedes the *Eschaton*. This is pretty straight Christian dogma, that there is a covenant between human beings and God Almighty and that the contract and the promise will be kept. I think it will be kept, and the challenge of science is to overcome its struggles with religion, and guide us into the presence of the *Eschaton* using the tools and the descriptive approaches that it has perfected. The proper attitude toward the *Eschaton* is not prayer and sacrifice alone. The proper attitude is inquisitive understanding, curiosity, and delighted anticipation. The end of history is an object in nature like the electron, the spiral galaxy, and the human body, "a complex nexus," to use Whitehead's words, of temporal complexity that accounts for our existence. Without the *Eschaton*, there would have been no human beings—no you, no me, no pyramids, no Stonehenge, no Catholic Church, no Hassidism—none of these things would exist. They are the precursive anticipation of the perfection that lies at the end of the morphogenetic process of self-expression that is history. We are a part of it in the sense that we represent the individual atoms that are flowing together to make the transcendental object at the end of time.

I'll put myself out of business long before 2012 if other people don't start seeing things my way, because part of the prophecy, if you will, is that awareness of this impending event will spread, not simply through those who take their inspiration from Gideon or Stropharia, but among those who study particle physics, temporal matrices, and general modeling of nature. Nature cannot be made sense of without this kind of a singularity. Science has recognized this, only putting the singularity out of reach and safely in the past. This doesn't explain organism, intelligence, or history. To do that, you have to take this mysterious moment of concrescent involutional totality and put it in the end state. It's a matter of simple logical necessity. The fact that it was achieved by psychedelically driven visionary shamanizing only shows how similar these two methods are in their conclusion.

RA: Terence, I'd like to consider this millennial obsession of yours in the context of a deep habit, a runnel in the morphic field of our civilization. We have habits of thinking about time. We have philosophies of time, and consideration of time according to certain models. The idea of time having a singularity at the beginning and a singularity at the end is one model of time, and, as Rupert has observed in the past, when you believe in the Big Bang, it's easier to believe that there's a singularity at the end.

TM: There's more evidence there's a singularity at the end.

RA: It seems to me that the situation is quite symmetrical, and neither the singularity at the end, nor the singularity at the beginning makes any difference. There's another model of time, the cyclical one, where we have the cycle of the four ages repeated indefinitely, with not only a Golden Age in the past, but a Golden Age in the future as well. The utopian Trinitarian model is a version of this laid down by Joachim di Fiore when he changed the classical four epoch model into a three epoch model to agree with the Christian trinity. These two habits, which account basically for the utopian and the millennial obsessions of the human species over this historical period of 6000 years, were enabled by certain mathematical models of time coming into consciousness. First, we must understand a line, then we think of a linear model of time, and then we understand circles as our mathematical consciousness grows. Recently we have had a proliferation of new models for time. You, for example, have contributed enormously to the history of the philosophy of time by creating a fractal model of time. Chaos theory, likewise, has given many new models for transformation, which transcend the singularity concepts. Our mathematical capability has evolved to a certain point where we can recognize many other forms of transformation in nature occurring through time. The New Age expectation is for a social transformation, a future history that is not boring. The dream of a social transformation has historical support. You said that history is the trumpet of the human experience. Compare our fantasy of what's going on with the historical record, we find that the historical record does not support the *Eschaton*. This is a particular interpretation based on a very archaic model, the oldest model of time in the history of consciousness.

TM: At the beginning you said that the two possibilities—a singularity at the beginning, or at the end of the process of universal becoming—these seem...

RA: Equally improbable, as you pointed out.

TM: I didn't say that. I said I think it's much more probable to find it at the end of a process, when you have great complexity, than to believe it would spring from a state of utter nothingness.

RA: The historical record is compatible with the idea of an upcoming, amazing, difficult, and creative social transformation in our immediate future. The future will not be boring. Transformation will be a chaotic transient from one attractor to another, a period of destabilization when all constraint of history is lifted, novelty is empowered to actually do something instead of being constantly frustrated, and then we wake up one morning and read in the paper that the sun is rising in a different way. This has happened in the past. It's in the historical record of people who wrote of history by whatever model, whether it's the cyclic model or the linear progressive model or whatever. History goes along boringly the same for a while, eventually there's a destabilization, then you have rapid change to a new equilibrium.

Among these different equilibria there is perhaps a kind of progression in the long run. In this model, catastrophic transformations are announced by plagues and disasters, and the dissolution of established structures, out of which, like a Phoenix from the ashes, comes a new organization which might be glorious. The longest view in this transformational model of history, is given in a history of our living Earth by Jim Lovelock, called *The Ages of Gaia*. In that book he describes the whole history of life on the planet as a series of equilibria punctuated by catastrophic transformations, eight really major transformations, the last one 65 million years ago.

TM: This shows the kind of attention he gives to human history.

RA: In this view, even the human species could disappear and life may be boring for microbes, but they will go on, the biosphere will not end, life is not over. Maybe the *Eschaton* is only for the human species.

TM: The reason I don't buy the idea that this is simply one more renaissance, or one more gothic revival, is because these breakthroughs to novelty are occurring faster and faster. It's not just that they happen, it's that they happen faster and with more frequency. Whatever James Lovelock's affinity for something happening 65 million years ago, a few things of high interest have happened since, like everything in the human world. When you look at human history and technology and the spread of peoples and genes and so forth, it's clear that we've reached some kind of limit. Maybe you get one more renaissance before you slam into the wall, but not a dozen, not a hundred. This is not the Renaissance, this is not the rise of Rome, this is the final global crisis. The objective data support me on this.

RS: But it's so provincial, Terence. There's a sense in which the millenarian vision is a product of the historical model that grew up within one branch of human consciousness: the Judaic-Christian-Islamic branch. There's a sense in which you could argue that all this is a kind of self-fulfilling prophecy. Having unleashed these millenarian visions, our history's been driven by millenarian visions, which actually empowered and directed the discovery of America, the opening up of the New World, the rise of science and technology, the development of the atom bomb. Most of the things that are actually creating the crisis are man-made.

Even if we collide into this wall of history here on Earth, I find it quite incredible that the rest of the solar system is just going to shut up shop and go out of business, let alone the galaxy, let alone the clusters of galaxies.

TM: Here's a man who thinks the sun is alive!

RS: The sun could undergo tremendous transformation. I'll concede the entire solar system to you. That leaves an awful lot else, like the rest of the galaxy.

TM: I'll take it...The galaxy can take care of itself.

RS: The question is whether we're talking about human destiny on Earth, or the destiny of Earth, or the destiny of the solar system? Or is this about the entire cosmos, countless trillions of galaxies, stars everywhere? I can't believe that the kind of transformation you're talking about, or even the implosion of the entire solar system, is going to set out more than the most minute ripples throughout even our own galaxy.

TM: Implicit in that objection is that you really believe that there are millions of light years of space and time filled with spiral galaxies. It could all be a screen. The true size of the cosmic stage is a hotly debated subject, even among the experts. When you say it's too local, then you attack the universalistic position. We only have two choices—either what you disdainfully call provincialism, or what you disdainfully call universalism. It's got to be one or the other. I'm uncomfortable with the universal thing myself. However, I'm also uncomfortable with the idea that the universe as described by Newtonian astronomers should go absolutely unchallenged. This anthropic principle that astronomers have begun to allow into their deliberations suggests that maybe the stars aren't as fixed in their courses as we imagine, and that somehow events on the earth could have a kind of cosmic significance.

RS: The apocalyptic tradition is more like Ralph's version. It's not everything suddenly disappearing in a blinding light. It's a period of transformation followed by the Millennium, a period in which the kingdom of heaven is realized on Earth. That is something that's lacking from your vision. You don't think beyond the year 2012.

I, like Ralph, am more inclined to traditional millenarianism, a transitional period followed by the kingdom of heaven on Earth. What I think this could involve is first of all, psychedelics; secondly, the revival of animism; thirdly, mathematical objects visible to all through computers; and fourthly, communication with the stars. Through conscious communication a network of consciousness begins to link up, far beyond the Earth, to other stars, other galaxies. A thousand years to effect this linking up of consciousness throughout the entire cosmos, at the end of which, the true and absolute *Eschaton* might be possible. Right now it would be confined to Earth, or at most the solar system.

TM: I think that the thousand years should be scaled back by orders of magnitude. It will be more like ten years. The thousand years prophecy was naive by virtue of being made in a different era with less compression of time. We will then build quite naturally toward the revelation of the *Eschaton* sometime around 2012.

*So the work on island dispersal patterns and the statistical me-
chanics of this process will eventually, I think, play a role in modeling how life is dispersed throughout the galaxy.*

CHAPTER 6

An Evolutionary Leap

*T*erence McKenna: In this conversation, I'd like to talk
about Hawaii, the island—what it tells us about evolution, and how it relates to island ecosystems and their evolutionary process. The task falls to me because as chance would
have it, in the course of my life I've visited most of the major
theaters of evolution on the planet that involve the exemplars
of the various types of island groups. Hawaii, where we are recording this trialogue, is a group of mid-ocean volcanic islands. The only other mid-ocean volcanic island groups in the
world are the Azores, the Canaries and the Seychelles. They
offer great contrast to Hawaii, particularly the Seychelles,
which as a portion of the Madagascar landmass has been
above water some 300 million years, perhaps longer than any
other place on the planet. There the evolutionary process offers a dramatic contrast to the far more recent evolution in the
Hawaiian Islands. The Hawaiian Islands represent the unique
case, because of the size of the volcanic calderas and of the
vents beneath the Pacific floor that have created them. In fact,
these vents and volcanic conduits are the largest on the planet. What we have in Hawaii is a tectonic plate sliding slowly
toward southern Russia and Japan that is crossing over a

weak place in the Earth's crust, a place where the core magma of the planet lies a considerable percentage closer to the surface than anywhere else on earth. The result of this situation is a series of islands formed in the same spot that each, after its volcanic birth, is rafted away on the continental plate towards the northwest.

The life in the Hawaiian Islands shows 30 to 35 million years of endemism using the ordinary rates of gene change that biologists recognize. Nevertheless, geologically speaking, no Hawaiian island is over 12 million years old. The obvious interpretation of these facts is that life arose out here on islands that no longer exist, and as islands rose and fell, the life hopscotched from one island to another. Indeed, the dispersal rate of birds, tree snails, and other organisms moving eastward from Kauai across Oahu, Molokai and Maui to the Big Island, Hawaii itself, shows that this gradient is still operable. The forests of Hawaii have the poorest amount of species in the major islands. Hawaii is species poor because animals are still arriving here from the other islands. Nevertheless because these volcanoes are so huge, Hawaii has a complete range of ecological systems, from sea level to 14,000 feet, virtually the entire range on the planet in which life is able to locate itself. The volcano itself, Mauna Loa, is by volume the world's largest mountain, because it is already a 14,000 foot mountain when it breaks through to sea level, having risen from the Pacific floor, and in this part of the world the Pacific Ocean is 13,000 feet deep. This mountain was enormous before it ever broke water. It now rises 13,000 feet above sea level, and its sister mountain, Mauna Kea, is shorter by only 120 feet.

What has been created out here is a very closed ecosystem far from any continental landmass. The forms of life that arise here arise on rafted debris or tucked into the feathers of migratory birds or in some other highly improbable fashion. What we see here is a winnowing of continental species based on extreme improbability. As an example, a very common Sierra Nevada wildflower of no great distinction apparently arrived millions of years ago as a single seed on Maui, and by that crossing has created a mutated race of plants that we know as the Hawaiian Silversword, one of the most bizarre endemic plants that the island has produced.

In terms of islands within islands and the fractal adumbration of nature, it's very evident here. For example, because the island is created by a series of lava flows of varying ages, there is a constant process in which ecosystems become islands by lava flows. And so you have a series of micro-islands of species that develop independently of each other even though they may only be some few miles apart, but separated by a landscape so toxic and desolate that there is very little intermixing of genes. This is thought to have been a formative factor in the evolution of the Hawaiian fruit flies, Drosophila. They of course were very useful in early studies of genetics because the chromosomes of the Hawaiian Drosophila are ten thousand times larger than the ordinary Drosophila. In the era before electron microscopes you could actually color band these with certain dyes.

In terms of extrapolating all of this particular natural history data into some sort of general model, I think what life on the island brings home to us is that the earth itself is an island. I've been saying for many years that one of the most revolutionary yet totally trivial and predictable revolutions sure to

come in biology is the recognition that models of island isolation or species dispersion across oceans can easily be expanded to the three-dimensional ocean of outer space.

Very clearly viruses, prions, gene fragments, molecularly
coded information, percolate between the stars as a statistically very low component of the general cosmic dust and debris. Indeed, there have been many attempts to establish this
idea, by Fred Hoyle and others. Recently a theory of the
cometary origin of life has been put forward. It seems to me
perfectly obvious that in time these notions will be embraced;
after all, viruses can freeze down to crystalline states that are
almost minerals. And as for dispersion between celestial bodies, it's now generally agreed that a number of meteorites that
have been recovered in the Antarctic are in fact fragments of
Mars. So the work on island dispersal patterns and the statistical mechanics of this process will eventually, I think, play a
role in modeling how life is dispersed throughout the galaxy.

Some of the other islands that I've been fortunate enough
to relate to are the Indonesian islands, which are the absolute
other end of the spectrum of the class of tropical islands. What
we have here in Hawaii, as I said, are mid-ocean islands far
from continental floras and faunas, while Indonesia is in fact
a submerged continent. As recently as 120,000 years ago, Indonesia, from Sumatra to New Guinea, was a single landmass
which paleobiologists refer to as Sundaland. In the process of
this shallow continent's subsidence, the sea filled in the low
spots, so that today there is a direct correlation between species differentiation on any two Indonesian islands and the
depth of the sea between them. This correlation has been
shown over and over. One of the great conundrums of nineteenth-century biology was the so-called problem of Wallace's

Line. Alfred Russel Wallace, co-discoverer with Darwin of the principle of natural selection, believed that between the islands of Bali and Lombok and then going west of Celebes you could draw a line which represented the line of convergence between the Austral-Papuan biogeographical zones and the Asian-Malayan zones.

Statistical studies, Ernst Mayr's principally, have disproved this notion. However, I have collected butterflies and stood in the forests on both sides of Wallace's Line in several places and I completely understand Wallace's observation and in fact wonder about Mayr's conclusion. Wallace concluded that these forests are very different; the bird calls, the butterflies, and the flora all seemed different. But what Mayr seemed to show was that there was no distinct line. There was a gradient from Australia to Malaya in one direction and Malaya to Australia in the other direction. Although I haven't mentioned the Galapagos, island groups like this are obvious laboratories of speciation. So much so that when Darwin and Wallace and Walter Henry Bates and other nineteenth-century biologists who were grappling with the so-called species problem set out to do their fieldwork, they could not fail to be impressed by this peculiar theme and variation. They could not understand whose fingers strung the harp until they realized that similar populations separated by catastrophe such as the arrival of ocean water or a lava flow, then come under very slightly different selection pressures which cause slightly different physical characteristics to be taken on. In the Amazon Basin for example, you can move 2,000 miles and have only about a 15% replacement in butterfly species. In Indonesia you can cross a strait of water 20 miles wide and have a 17% replacement of butterfly species. Darwin and Wallace visited these places, both continental floras and faunas and the island situations, and through careful observation they finally understood what the mechanism of speciation was. And it's a wonderful thing, you know. Take for example butterfly diversity, that is a situation where diversity itself confers adaptive advantage. Because birds largely predate upon butterflies, it's been shown in numerous studies that birds hunt a target image. They have an image of their prey. If through the chance recombination of genes your wing color or wing shape pushes you outside the target spectrum, you will be ignored and survive.

Ralph Abraham: Like us!

TM: And so variety itself becomes a premium in the evolutionary game. Novelty itself then is preserved because novelty confers an adaptive advantage in this situation, for birds and butterflies. I think the implications of these things lie close to the surface. Earth is a small island, we are making great changes in its ecological parameters, and we are affecting plant and animal populations. By studying how evolution has shaped island groups, we can appreciate our own small cosmic island and perhaps eventually draw politically empowering conclusions from that.

Rupert Sheldrake: What a wonderful overview, Terence! A real delight.

There remains a major evolutionary puzzle. Islands have a tremendous role in speciation, as all evolutionists believe. Both Darwin and Wallace provided classic examples. Then in places where there are contacts through island chains the flora can be extremely rich in species, as in the Malaysian-Indo-nesian archipelago, one of the great creation centers of species in the world. That's the kind of tropical forest I know best, having lived in Malaysia. From what you've said, this evolutionary creativity arises from a combination of isolation on islands, plus mingling of two totally radically different floras, giving rise to all sorts of new possibilities and combinations.

TM: And the process was pumped by the repetitive comings and goings of the sea, which repeatedly created island populations and then reunited them.

RS: And presumably also pumped by the ice ages not only through changes in sea level, but also through the compression of all forms of life towards the tropics, followed by a poleward migration of species at the end of each ice age. All this makes sense for the center of evolutionary creativity in the Malaysian-Indonesian archipelago. The problem is that it doesn't explain that other great center of evolutionary creativity, the Amazon basin.

TM: The answer is very simple. It has simply been above ground a very long time. In other words, the Malaysian-Austro-Papuan situation is fairly recent; probably the map has looked as it does no more than seven or eight million years. The Amazon on the other hand has been above water 280 to 300 million years. So simply being in the tropics with three, four, five breeding seasons a year for many organisms, and never being inundated by seawater or catastrophe allowed that incredible climatic speciation on a continental landmass.

You're right, it didn't happen as far as we know in Africa, although Africa's so heavily impacted by human beings that any notion of its original natural history is impossible. But that's the short answer, that it was above water a long, long time.

RS: But then we have two methods of prolific evolution. One depends on being around a long time, as in the case of the Amazon. The other depends on isolation, climatic pumping, mixing of gene pools and so on.

TM: What pumped the Amazon situation on a micro level is the meandering of rivers. You see, it's very hard in a climaxed forest situation for any new species to gain a foothold. But because rivers meander and destroy forests and create sandbars and the intermediate zone of uninhabited land, so-called pioneer species can move in there. And that's where the speciation is taking place. Carl Sauer estimated that before the advances of human culture it was the meandering rivers that were the main force for modern plant evolution on this planet. A vast amount of shifting of boundaries goes on, and it's in that shifting boundary zone that mutants, new forms, can get hold. That's why a pioneer plant species will have the following characteristics. It will be an annual and it will be a prolific seeder. It will be herbaceous, not woody. In short, it will be a weed. And that's what a weed is, a pioneer species, a tremendously predatory species designed for open land, utterly unable to compete in the forest, but in open land able to take over very well.

RS: Yes, but while isolation, new environments and so on, explain one side of evolution, I think there's another side which

Darwinism can't explain, because it puts too much emphasis on natural selection. J.C. Willis, the great British botanist who worked in Ceylon and knew the Asian flora well started off as a keen Darwinian, but was forced to the conclusion that much evolution took place by divergent mutation, rather than natural selection. For example, in Ceylon and India there are many species of water plants in the family Podostemaceae that live in streams with leaves that float on water, with many different leaf forms. Any attempt to account for a particular leaf form in terms of adaptation to water flow fails because leaves of quite different shape seem to do just as well, and can flourish side by side.

TM: Well, the Hawaiian Hapu here is an excellent example. Here we have the two tree ferns, two distinct species, distributed in a ratio of 50-50. One has little black stems with stickers and the other has a fuzzy brown soft stem. What selective pressure caused stickers to work for one and not to work for the other, when they're standing right next to each other? Seems to me there must be drift of genes or simply variety for its own sake.

RS: Life is constantly trying out new forms. Unsuccessful novelties are weeded out by natural selection. A few are a wild success. But many novel forms may work equally well, and survive equally well, like the two species of tree ferns in your Hawaiian forest. There may just be lots of equivalent species, where you've got novelty for novelty's sake. They are not all closely shaped and sculpted by natural selection.

RA: Well, getting back to Hawaii here, it seems, if I understood you right, that what's unique about Hawaii is the Hawaiian Islands are young, and they're maximally oceanic islands, far from any continents. And the process of the population of a new island from a neighboring island is visible, even in the present, and then we see a certain pattern is repeated over and over again, even in the course of a century. So it seems to me that these different examples you were talking about conflate two different processes more or less projected upon the same screen. One is a purely biogeographical process that could at least be imagined to be operating the same way without any evolution. We have only the same species that were found on Maui suddenly appearing on Hawaii by a process of dispersal. Some species are successful at pioneering, and help create an ecology suitable for the second species, and their space-time patterns are developed one upon another, very interesting fractal movies that to begin with would have nothing to do with evolution.

On top of that, you have—I'm not sure about the relative time scales of this—then you have an evolutionary process involving speciation either during or after the colonization of a brand new island. Is evolutionary process essential to the population of the new island or isn't it?

TM: I think in the short term it isn't and in the long term it is. Because many forms of life are arising in these islands, it's not home free. New arrivals must contend with this kind of island-making by volcanic flow that I mentioned, and other large-scale catastrophic events that have gone on in the Hawaiian Islands. Basically I think that what we see here are genes being mixed and stirred at a faster rate than in most places and that's without mentioning the vast number of plants and animal introductions brought by human beings. One of the other unique things about Hawaii that I didn't enumerate is that human beings arrived late and this absence of long-term human impact gives us a clearer picture of what's happening. It's almost as though Hawaii is a speeded up microcosm of the earth itself, probably eight-tenths of the big island is in the pre-archeozoic phase— in other words, almost abiotic—and then large areas are covered by lichen, with a fern or two here in the crevasses.

RA: You used the word *pumping*, and I like that. There's a sort of a forcing or coupling or a codependence between these different processes, physical ones, as for example new lava flows, the meandering of rivers, or the appearance of islands, and space/time evolutionary processes.

TM: Really the ice ages are the pump. They raise and lower sea levels. They create deserts and drop humidity. They force change. And they are probably driven by fluctuations in the dynamics of the sun.

RS: The evolutionary process looks rather different if you take morphic resonance into account. Habit formation then becomes a much more important evolutionary process. Individual organisms adapt to new environments. You can take seeds from a given plant and grow them at different altitudes and in different climates, and in many places they survive. But in these different environments, the plants grow differently. Grow them there over several generations and they develop a new group habit, stabilized by morphic resonance, without the need for genetic change.

TM: Well, adaptive behavior is that small margin of adjusting that supposedly is not genetically driven.

RS: Habit formation and the inheritance of these habits by morphic resonance could enable evolution to occur much more rapidly than neo-Darwinians suppose possible, because they ascribe almost everything to slow statistical changes in gene frequencies. Instead of mere random mutation and natural selection, you have the positive adaptation of animals and plants themselves to a new environment. They often react and respond in a creative way, forming new habits of life appropriate to the environment. So the creative adaptation of life to new circumstances, in my view, is not a matter of minor adjustments. What we are seeing is the innate creativity of life in action. Not blind random mutation, not just physical forces, not just natural selection, but a creativity inherent in all life. Morphic resonance would enable these new habits to be stabilized and inherited.

This theory suggests that not only can habits be passed on by morphic resonance from generation to generation, but also by morphic resonance forms and habits could jump from place to place. This could, for example, help to account for the parallel evolution of marsupials in Australia with placental mammals on other continents.

TM: It would augment the natural selection of separated genes in general.

RS: Yes, these things work together. There's still natural selection of gene pools; but creative adaptation and spread of new habits take place as well. I suppose the thing about Hawaii that puzzles me most is why there haven't been more species and more forms of life in Hawaii. In the rainforest here we see only half a dozen or so species of tree, whereas in Sumatra or in the Amazon, there would be hundreds.

TM: Again, the answer is time—200, 300 million years versus 20 million years. That's what it is.

RA: There are so many reasons to fail here. I personally find the environment harsh, lush as it may look to you or other people, and I suppose that one way a new species could fail is through having bad habits. There may be habits that manifest visually to us only in terms of spatial patterns. The colonization of the black lava by the Ohia tree appears in a certain fractal pattern in which there are characteristic frequencies of distances that may have to do with the distance the seeds fly in the wind or something like that. It could just be response to a nutrient because of the change in size and therefore characteristic distance in the space/time patterns. We seem to see that—first we see the lichen, the lichen creates just a minimum of degradation of the surface that makes it possible for the Ohia tree to grab hold. Both the lichen and the lava surface are fractal. And fractal means that there's a resonance across scales. Then the lichen scale, which is much smaller—there may be many kinds of lichen, but only this one grows because its fractal pattern has the right basic form, something like a time wave—so that as a matter of fact it's compatible with the bare rock. And then the Ohia tree is compatible with its fractal pattern apparently on a much larger scale, which nevertheless resonates harmoniously as opposed to other species that might be disharmonious. And this harmony, this capability of a certain space/time pattern, is a habit, which may change and adapt in a way that requires no change in DNA at all, a nongenetic variation, just dependent on some kind of morphic field.

RS: You are talking about the evolution and development of whole ecosystems. I think what's interesting about this island, the Big Island of Hawaii, is that this forest ecosystem gets established on the slopes of the volcano, but is wiped out again and again through new lava flows. When lava flows are recolonized, an entire ecosystem has to move not just single species. So it has to be an exceptionally portable ecosystem. Maybe that's why it has to travel light.

TM: Good point.

RA: Coming back to this question of the morphogenetic field of an entire ecosystem, I just want to ask you about this. In this creation myth of the Hawaiian Island's ecosystem that you described, there are islands that have already disappeared and ecosystems have jumped from them onto Kauai and so on. But as I understand it, these islands are rafting along over this more or less stationary hot spot. Those early islands were right here where we are sitting today, also very distant from any continental landmass. So is Day One of biology on the Hawaiian Island chain a result of long-distance dispersion?

TM: Yes.

RA: Nothing happened until the right lichen arrived after millions of years?

TM: Well the lichen I suspect can probably be found in air samples above any point on the planet.

RS: Say you've got spores as the first colonizers.

TM: Yes, and then the ferns come next, which also propagate by spores. The reason the nonflowering plants conquered the planet, if you think about it, is because the planet was like Hawaii. It was new lava, it was covered with lava flows, and the ferns could get hold. We think of ferns as soft, somehow spoiled plants. Actually, they're the toughest plants there are. When we study biology they teach you about *Psilotum*, related to the ancestors of the ferns. The forest here is full of Psilotum plants. I can point them out to you; they're tough.

RA: But how do they get here? Birds carry these spores?

TM: Well sure, by spores. Mud on the feet of migratory birds could carry millions of spores.

RS: The duck's foot theory. More necessary for the transport of seeds than spores, which are so small and so light that they can be carried over long distances in the air.

RA: Well I think there's a startup problem. I just can't imagine that the frequency of ducks flying is enough to explain the arrival of correct species and in the correct temporal sequence. I mean they would have to be dumping literally dump-truck loads of different genetic materials on a daily basis on a brand new island in order to have a chance to get started.

TM: No, studies with banded birds show that there's a lot of material moving around and a million years is a long time, a number of improbable things can go on in a million years.

RA: Well I've been here for a week. I have not seen a new species of bird arrive from the mainland.

TM: Well stick around.

RS: Okay, let's accept the duck's foot hypothesis, especially in relation to migratory birds. Birds do migrate from place to place over large distances, including many species in Hawaii, which has migrants from different continents. But which is cause and which is effect? No one knows the evolutionary basis for migration.

TM: No, I don't think it is migratory birds. I think the process is primarily one of a novelty, unusual events, and catastrophe. The greatest storm of the century, every century.

RA: Birds blown off course.

TM: Birds blown off course. Now that happens. A single big storm veering off course might equal a century of ordinary dispersal.

RS: But there are far more regular migrants. And migratory patterns of birds evolve. For example, new ones have appeared in Europe in a matter of a few decades, as in the case of the blackcap. Birds of this species that nest in Germany and Austria traditionally migrate in the winter to the western Mediterranean. But over the last 30 years, an ever-increasing proportion migrates to England instead, where they find abundant food on garden bird tables.

But how would species of migrants find out about Hawaii in the first place? Rather than individuals being blown here by chance or whole flocks of them starting out lemming-like from the coast of California in the hope of finding an island 2,500 miles away, they may in some way have known that there were islands there to go to. Perhaps this could happen through a kind of collective map that they share with other migratory birds. Some migratory species knowing about Hawaii may enable others to start off in that direction to follow a kind of pre-existing flight path rather like airline flight paths. On our flight to Hawaii, there was a vapor trail outside the window about a hundred feet away, which we followed exactly for two hours. It was presumably from the previous jet flight to Hawaii.

Maybe in bird migrations many species follow the same path, as many northwestern European species follow the Mediterranean coast of Spain and cross over the Straits of Gibraltar into North Africa, and North American migrants tend to follow four main north-south "flyways."

Maybe when the Hawaiian Islands appeared, long-distance migrants like albatrosses or other large seabirds noticed them and started coming here. Somehow this got into a general bird navigation map, and other species started coming.

The appearance of new land channeled bird migration routes towards it. The word got around and increasing numbers of species started coming here if only to rest on the way across the Pacific. Then the ducks' foot hypothesis would be very plausible.

RA: A new island in the Pacific, tell the albatrosses, and the birds do their job as sort of a pack train to bring as much genetic material as rapidly as possible and dump it on the new island.

RS: Somewhat like an adventure of Doctor Doolittle. But the question of how migratory birds found Hawaii raises the further question of the original Polynesian people who found it. One possibility is that they were keen observers of migrant birds and noticed that birds set off from their islands in a particular direction and months later came back again. It would therefore be a fairly simple deduction that if you followed the migrant birds you'd reach land sooner or later.

TM: That's right.

RA: That's what "East is a big bird" means. But following the birds is no less of a mystery than the birds themselves being able to migrate. So either the people could follow the birds, which navigate by some unknown mysterious means, or the people could have had access to similar mysterious means themselves. So when a new island comes up, then the information is somehow injected into their own migration patterns in their canoe rides from one island to another.

RS: In terms of human migration, these islands are now the limit of the westward migration of Europeans, having gone right across North America, subjugating the natives and trying to eliminate their culture, the whole process has moved here. We can see it happening before our very eyes, and in evolutionary terms it's the opposite of everything we've been talking about so far. Now there's no separation of the islands from the TV networks and other cultural forces of America.

TM: One of the most frightening trends I think in modern culture is the wish to build shopping malls everywhere. There is a mentality that would like to turn the entire planet into an international airport arrival concourse. That's someone's idea of Utopia.

RA: There appears to be a double gradient here with the eastward migration of Asian people balancing the westward migration of European people. This is actually the interface where the double gradient can produce an increase in novelty and new mutations, and a forward leap perhaps, of human evolution, could begin here.

TM: A standing wave forming here as forces move both east and west.

RS: So can we point to any human creativity in Hawaii that exemplifies the cultural equivalent of the Malaysian Archipelago? Or is it more like a stalemate with roughly half of the island's population coming from the East and half from the West, with the native Hawaiians trapped in between?

TM: Well, a Pacific Rim culture is hypothesized to be emerging, and Hawaii is central to all of that. It's equidistant from Sydney, Lima, Tokyo, and Vancouver.

RS: Have they adopted the slogan, "Hawaii, the Pacific Hub"?

TM: If they haven't, I'm sure they're not far behind. The presence of the world's largest telescopes here makes it a world center of astronomical science. I think the world's first, second and third largest telescopes are on this island, with an identical twin of the largest being built 200 yards away from it.

RS: So it's a center for linking humanity with the stars.

TM: We're looking out from the top of Hawaii, chosen paradoxically for being the darkest place on earth.

RA: From here they'll see the next wave of ducks' feet departing for Biosphere II.

People accept an incredible variety of things that are denied by science, such as astrology. But the scientific community, I think, would resist the proof, no matter how rigorous, because the scientific system is so inflexible, so closed to novelty, that it's essentially a dead end.

What we might be doing is not proving that telepathy is an invisible connecting web between everything, rather what we might be uncovering is but one more example of how language and cultural boundaries prevent us from correctly appreciating how nature works.

CHAPTER 7

PSYCHIC PETS

Rupert Sheldrake: I've been doing research on pets that suggests that many of them are psychic. Millions of people have dogs and cats that seem to know when they are coming home. The animal will go to the door, window or gate to wait for them coming home, often ten minutes or more before they arrive. This happens even when they are not expected, and even if they come home at irregular times. Many people have told me that they know when their partner is on the way home because of the behavior of the animal, and often start cooking a meal accordingly. The pet's anticipation of the arrival of the absent one is often both appreciated, and taken for granted. No one seems to think about it much, beyond assuming that it must be some kind of psychic or telepathic ability.

This kind of behavior is surprisingly common. In most groups of ten or more people I've been in, there's at least one person who has a personal experience of this anticipatory behavior of pets.

Once this phenomenon is brought to consciousness, it turns out to be a widely accepted item of common sense. In Britain, stories about this research have been featured in many newspapers and magazines, ranging from the *London Times* to *Dogs Today*, and I have had thousands of letters and emails from people telling me of the seemingly psychic powers of their pets.

In a BBC radio discussion on this subject, I was confronted with a notoriously witty but hard-bitten panel. I was expecting a skeptical response. The most formidable of the panelists simply said, "Well, my dog's been doing it for years." and the others duly added their own stories. His conclusion was: "The only thing that puzzles me about this behavior is why Dr. Sheldrake feels he needs to prove it."

In many cases, it turns out that the pets are responding to the time when the owner sets out from the place that they're leaving from to go home. In some cases, at my request, people have left at randomly selected times. And pets can still respond when the person comes home in an unusual way, for example by bicycle or in a taxi.

The experiments have shown that this is a real phenomenon, that it's common, and that research on it can be done very cheaply. What I would like to explore with you are the implications of this pet behavior.

Ralph Abraham: I agree with you that this is a sphere in which experiments could be very rewarding, and let's suppose that this effect is established convincingly. Then the question is how could this evoke a transformation of science?

I think that—this is just a pessimistic view from an optimist—this could be established and become commonplace but not significantly change the paradigm of culture at large, because there is already a huge space for what's called superstition. People accept an incredible variety of things that are denied by science, such as astrology. But the scientific community, I think, would resist the proof, no matter how rigorous, because the scientific system is so inflexible, so closed to novelty, that it's essentially a dead end.

This is pretty pessimistic, because science can't change and people don't need to change and no matter what is achieved in this most exemplary and promising of all possible experiments and domains, there wouldn't be any change in the world at large. However, for me personally, if I become convinced, or even without being convinced if I take seriously that pets and owners are able to exchange messages over distances, then this is really phenomenal. It moves along all my ideas. I mean, what this signifies is that everything is interconnected to a much stronger degree than anyone has been willing to admit.

RS: Except most people, when they are talking about their pets.

RA: Well, even if they have convincing experiences with their own pets, they probably cannot stretch to consider the possibility that all pets and people are connected.

Terence McKenna: Ralph, I think you make a good point about flexibility of the mass mind and the margin of superstition, but I think you're making the point too strongly. In other words, science is rigid, yes, but it isn't the Kabala. In other words, presented with sufficiently overwhelming evidence, scientists have no choice but to retreat. The word proved is tossed around—the thing is proved when one's enemy retires bloody and whimpering. Then it's proved. And we're not yet at the point where we should be so pessimistic. In other words, if 5 out of 30 ordinary people are reporting this, and then it turns out that it's actually real for 1 in 300, it could become an overwhelming argument. Quantum physics had to accept electron tunneling because the electrons kept coming through the energy barrier even though the equation said they didn't have enough oomph to get through. And so science had to make a place in theory for the utterly miraculous fact that apparently particles can sometimes move through energy barriers with impunity.

But I am skeptical. There are a number of things that went through my mind listening to this. It is certainly true that human beings and the two species that were mentioned, dogs and cats, have been in association for a very long time, in the case of dogs maybe half a million years. Not domesticated, but in the same environment, predating the same animals, and so on. In the case of dogs and humans, I would wager dogs are better candidates for this ability than cats. Many cats barely lift their heads when you walk in the front door. But dogs do seem to have this ability. Dogs and cats are social creatures that have evolved complex signals; so are human beings. They were very similar to us for a long time, but then the signal producing capacity of human beings evolved and the dogs were not really able to follow. It seems to me that behind shaman-ism is the idea that human and animal consciousness can be very closely intertwined and traded off. It's unproven, but certainly a commonplace of fringe speculation, that in the prehistoric human past, human beings were telepathic with each other. This suggests that early human beings may have been telepathic with their animals, that they may have had a relationship with their animals that precedes what we view as rational.

Having said all that, then I take a different position. When Rupert described the phenomenon and you responded to it, there was a kind of implicit assumption that we understand how this works. We think we've arrived at the new paradigm, that this phenomenon between pets and their friends is telepathy, that this is the proof of the existence of an invisible field, an influence that links everything together, that in fact if this could be proven it could be the centerpiece of our model for wholeness. And yet all of that rests on the utterly unproven assumption that we know how the phenomenon works. It could very well be that we have a misapprehension of causality — I've argued this in other trialogues. And that the reason the dog knows when you're going to be home is because the dog doesn't exactly live in the same "now" that has been created by culturally-defined human language. Nature does not exist in the Newtonian now that we exist in. It's much more a wave-mechanical field of consciousness. The past is the trailing edge of the wave; the future is the leading edge of the wave. Plasticity is in the moment. So that what we might be doing is not proving that telepathy is an invisible connecting web between everything, rather what we might be uncovering is but one more example of how language and cultural boundaries prevent us from correctly appreciating how nature works.

RA: We try to map experience into language, but we must admit that in mapping it into language, into a popular process, we strip it of 90 percent of its meaning.

TM: For example, when I suggested that this phenomenon might be based on field theory I was suggesting that it would be found to be subject to the inverse square law. These are predictions we can make about this phenomenon if we accept a certain type of describable mechanism. So that's the way to proceed, hypothesize the mechanism, see what cases it mimics, see if those cases apply, further refine, so forth and so on. Then you'll have the outline of a model.

RS: My model is that these connections between pets and their owners depend on a morphic field similar to the morphic fields around flocks of birds or around packs of wolves, the fields of social groups. Dogs adopt human beings as honorary members of the pack and form social bonds with them just as wolves do with each other. That's the biological background. These morphic fields connect things together in the present and are sustained by their memory from the past. Morphic fields also contain attractors, which draw organisms towards future states. When people are going home, the home is the attractor in their field. Getting home is their goal, their intention, and the dog somehow picks up this change in the field, and knows they are on the way.

TM: The leading edge of the probabilistic waves of happenstance.

RS: Something like that would be my model. But there are already phenomena that this model can't cope with—for example the precognitive powers of pets, apparently foreseeing disasters, giving warnings of earthquakes, and so on. Many pets living in London during the Second World War gave warnings of air raids 20 minutes or more before the warning sirens went off, so their owners were always first into the air raid shelters. Some dogs even responded in advance to the approach of the supersonic V2 rockets the Germans were shooting at London. Since these were supersonic, it doesn't seem likely that dogs could have heard them, does it?

TM: Well these things have a relationship to time, as I'm suggesting.

RS: They do. That's why I mention them. They fit your model better than mine.

RA: No, no. Terence's model is very compatible with yours. At least if you take the word resonance seriously, thinking of wave motion. The wave motion doesn't happen in instantaneous time. It requires an extended field in space and time. There's a minimum extent where wave motion could even be recognized by another wave motion, so an interlocking of little space-time patterns over a significant region of space and time is implied the minute you use the word resonance, and that's exactly what Terrence is talking about. All these phenomena have extension in time, that the early part of one extension in time is a wave packet that could interlock with the latter part of another wave and then together construct a kind of a model, and this is probably the simplest way to encompass precognition in the context of morphogenetic fields or morphic resonance.

RS: Thank you. This is a breakthrough. But a lot would depend on the frequency of the rhythm. One is a daily rhythm. Daily cycles of sleeping and waking are the basis of a day-to-day resonance, and this could lead to precognitive effects a few hours in advance, maybe a few days in advance. And indeed, most human premonitions, as in dramatic warning dreams about impending plane crashes or other disasters, appear to relate to events minutes, hours or at most a few days in advance. The same is true of premonitions by pets. But the more distant the premonition, the longer the underlying resonant wavelet, with wavelets of human generations, or of the rise and fall of empires, and even of vast Gaian cycles like the ice ages. And I suppose these long-term resonances usually claim less attention than the short term.

TM: That's why you only get one Nostradamus, and every dog or cat can tell you what's going on ten minutes in the future.

RA: Well this brings up the whole question of morphic wavelets. I don't know if we've discussed morphic wavelets.

RS: Not yet, no.

RA: Wavelets are a wonderful new way of looking at vibratory phenomena in general and a way that's very compatible with the ideas of fractal geometry. Because you have a basic wave-let that you add together to make big waves, and they differ not just in frequency but also as a matter of scale, sort of an amplitude of scale and so on. This very way of looking gives a mother morphic wavelet which, through changing its scale only, you reproduce smaller and larger morphic wavelets. The addition of these together with different amplitudes as it were makes a big wave pattern.

RS: A fractal wave pattern.

RA: Well, the very fact that vibrations might be made of wavelets in this way gives a reason why you might expect there to be similarities across scales when you look from the perspective of fractal geometry. So if we have a wave, let's say, a morphic space-time pattern characterizing a thought such as a historical event like a bomber coming, and that wave has a resonance with the mind wave of a pet, and these waves are in a resonance process. This would probably involve one or two favorite wavelets that are components of the big waves of history. A favorite wave more or less compatible and more resonant, as it were, with the mental vibratory fields of that pet. Therefore there could be some specialist of two-day pre-cognition and another specialist of two-year precognition and so on, that has to do with your wavelet spectrum. Morphic wavelets.

RS: But how can there be resonance with waves yet to come?

RA: Well, think of a wave packet that's traveling along and it has a certain extension in time and some of them have a bigger extension in time.

RS: Like day waves.

RA: For example, today's frequency. A day wavelet would be one that an insect that lives for a day would have a great deal of difficulty in making resonance with. They would specialize in the higher frequencies.

TM: This is essentially exactly how the time wave works.

RA: Exactly. That's what I'm saying. I see an overlap in your views here under which I'm now going to fan the flame.

TM: But Rupert, I wanted to ask you, what does this say about communication between animals and their owners?

RS: Well, morphic resonance cannot in itself explain how a pet anticipates its owner's return. Pets can respond by going to wait for their owner at the time they set off to come home from many miles away, even at a completely nonroutine time. Morphic resonance is primarily an influence from the past, and would play a general role in stabilizing the field or bond between the pet and the owner. But most of my current experiments are to do with the spatial aspects of morphic fields. I now see from the nice way Ralph has put them together that I had been separating too much in my own mind the temporal and the spatial aspects of morphic fields

TM: Well, all traditions of transcendence and asceticism put a great deal of stock on silence, isolation, contemplation, meditation, and the payoff is supposed to be the ability to access some vast, more complete and spiritually holistic level of nature. Perhaps we have literally fallen out of time and into history. History is a kind of damming of animal time that exists underneath the aegis of language, spoken language, while the rest of nature abides in a very different dimension, and all the things that are so mysterious to us, that appear to violate causality or action at a distance, these things have to do with the fact that, far more than we realize, we are the victims of a false perception of time created by our languages, our alphabet. I don't know exactly what is causing it, but it is obvious that in nature we are uniquely the prisoners of language.

RA: Do you mean that the rest of nature has more time?

TM: The rest of nature can see its termination in the *Eschaton*.

RS: How so?

TM: Well, Plato said time is the moving image of eternity. Let's change two words and say history is the moving image of biology. We are in history. It's all about process; it's all about where we've been, where we're going, where we are. It's this sector that's moving through space/time. Meanwhile, we access hyperspace through psychedelics and assume that nature abides outside of history. Don't we?

RS: No we don't. We think of nature in evolutionary development, and as having a history revealed by the fossil record.

TM: Well by our scale it's static. Ultimately you're right. You can't feel the Earth move and yet we know it moves, and I don't think you can feel biology's historicity, even though evolution teachers us it has historicity. But what language reveals is the frantic inner dynamic of ourselves, and immersion in it has caused us to have a profound bifurcation from our interior and exterior experience of time.

RA: Well why should language have a function of separating us from history and eternity?

TM: Because it lies.

RA: It has tenses, past, present and future.

TM: But it's particular. And nature is not particular. You can never understand nature as long as you particularize it, and language cannot do otherwise.

RS: But nature is particulate. For example flowers of the lily family have petals arranged in groups of three. The petals, sepals and other parts of flowers are quantized.

RA: They're very particulate.

TM: Now what we're doing here is we're talking fractals.

RA: I think this language should somehow be capable of imaging the extension and interconnection of all and everything, but maybe language as it evolves in our context has somehow become impoverished in those metaphors while emphasizing others.

TM: It has. This is why we're all so attracted to visual technology. Language is an impoverished metaphor. I think we sense that the way out of the language trap is through the image.

RA: What about musical experience? It's an antithesis of all this language restriction. Most people listen to music on the radio or on recordings for quite a bit of time every day. And this experience transcends language. We don't have any words for the musical experience and yet we have no trouble. We can recognize songs that we've heard before and so on. And a song can't be recognized from a single note. You need the entire sequence. And that is not an eternity, but a fairly long temporal extension of a song that fits into our cognitive apparatus.

TM: I think outside of our linguistic programming, sound is light, and light is sound. Somehow inside our linguistic and neurological programming there'd been a bifurcation of this processing.

RA: Maybe language was originally like music. You have the song and the lyrics, and then after the song was dropped off by accident you had the lyrics standing by themselves. The Vedas were chanted rather than read. I've been reading about the pronunciation of ancient Greek, as reconstructed by classical scholars. It sounds like singing. Greek poetry was orated. Nobody read a poem. It was later on that people got in the habit of silent reading, reading a book without saying anything. So this degeneration of musical language into dumb speech is something very recent in our evolution. There is so much we've forgotten, so difficult to recover.

TM: That's why an archaic revival is indicated.

RA: The song is actually prelinguistic language. A prelinguistic history that is actually linguistic in the sense of communicative music goes way back into Homo Erectus prehistory. And when we're talking about the communication between dogs and their owners, then maybe this is about a rediscovery in the deep unconscious of these prelinguistic modes, which are the natural modes of the mental field.

TM: The Australian Aborigines say that one sings the world into existence.

RS: Singing doesn't usually play a very explicit part in the relationship between dogs and their owners.

TM: No, but no human has as much experience with dogs from prehistory as the Australian Aborigines. And they're very much the keepers of this gnosis of a dreamtime, an alternative dimension outside of history. It's all about modes of time. If you perceive time in this a-historical mode, then what returns to you is a nature become alive, full of intent, intelligence, and information. If you don't have that view of time nature becomes dead, a resource for exploitation. Don't you think?

RA: Oh I think that dogs chant sometimes. They sing to music, they howl at night. Coyotes howl in choruses between different packs all through the night. And it could be that with the way we're speaking with our pets it's actually the music that they're getting.

TM: I recall that Robert Graves tried to make a case that there was a kind of Ursprach, a primary poetic language that directly addresses the emotions. That human emotions could be addressed through shamanic poetry. He traced the function of language back deeper and deeper into the function of a poem, and what poetry seeks to evoke.

RS: Yes, quite. But what dogs and cats seem to pick up are intentions. They pick up when people are about to go away on holiday even before they've started packing. They pick up when people want to take them to the vet, and will often hide. Dogs often pick up when they're going to be taken for a walk. Dogs can be trained to respond not just to words and whistles, but even to silent, mental commands. Many dogs and cats seem to know when a person they are bonded to has died, even when this happens far away. They seem to be sensitive to changes in the field that connects them to their people. This field is affected by the activities, emotions and intentions of their people—whether they're coming back or going away, whether they've died, whether they're in pain or trouble, whether they want to play. The animals seem to be picking up not specific messages but rather general changes in the tension of the field...

RA: In the mental field.

RS: Mental is perhaps not the right word. The field concerned is a social field, interrelating animals to each other, as in a flock of birds or people and animals, as in the case of pets and their human families.

TM: It's always said that shamans can talk to the animals and that animals will come to visit a shaman. I've even heard stories of contemporary Ayahuasca groups where deer and raccoons would practically overrun the group in the night, come to join the circus.

RA: I think when you begin to take these ideas seriously then I'm going to see you become a true vegetarian.

TM: But Ralph, the most intelligent entities we know are plants.

RS: One thing that we haven't explored much is the evolutionary connections between people and animals. Long before animals were domesticated, people were paying close attention to wild animals, if only so they could hunt them more effectively. And long before people appeared on the scene, predator and prey in general must have had a close interrelationship. And their responses to each other must have evolved, and must have been subject to natural selection.

TM: Human beings occupy an interesting position in all of this because until fairly recently the evidence suggests we were vegetarians, fruit-eating, canopy-living creatures, and then we became omnivores and began to predate small animals. There is no reason why a vegetarian animal should pay any attention to the behavior of other animal species. But for a predator, it's very important to study the behavior of your prey, and that study actually represents a kind of identification with the prey. This process could have been an impulse toward the evolution of consciousness, the need to model the behavior of other animals mentally in order to obtain them for dinner. A horse, a cow, they don't do that. But certainly hunting animals exhibit what we naively call intelligence.

RA: I think there is a reason for vegetarians to communicate carefully with other animal species and that has to do with the competition for resources. We have a tree full of fruit, the mongooses like to eat this fruit, and if they get it first then we won't have any. So we have to know when the mongooses are on their way to steal the fruit.

TM: But if you were a monkey competing with mongooses for fruit, you wouldn't study the behavior of mongooses, you'd study the fruiting habits of fruit trees.

RA: To get there first. But you would still want to know where the competitors are, how far away they are, and how much time have you got to harvest the fruit. And if you are a hungry predator, to catch an animal you want to eat, you have to know where it is even though it's not visible.

TM: It may be that the shamanic link between humans and animals is that consciousness was at first not self-conscious. It was consciousness of others, of food. It's only later that this consciousness moved into a position of self-identity within the psychic structure. The earliest conscious creatures were not conscious that they were conscious. They were conscious that the food was conscious.

RA: There's no evolutionary advantage to self-consciousness, is there? What good is it, self-consciousness?

RS: One theory is that its origins are social. In intensely bonded social groups, internalizing the behavior of others, and learning how to predict their moods and behaviors, is of great advantage.

RA: So self-consciousness is actually a degenerate form of the consciousness of a flock field.

RS: It's a form where you get intense individualized or personalized interactions within the group, as in small groups of eight or so. You have an internalized model of others who become part of your world. They have an internalized model of you. And through modeling others, you acquire an ability that can later be used to model yourself. It's like what Terence was saying about predators modeling the prey, but it's now modeling other members of the social group, and then modeling one's self.

TM: But a shaman is the person who has great ability to communicate with animals, even at a distance, because the shaman's chief function is to locate the game. How simple that could be if he could look at the world through the eyes of the prey. A shaman is definitely a specialist in human-animal communication and in that sense perhaps closer to a prelinguistic state of mind. So that as the rest of the society socializes, bonds together in tight groups using ordinary speech, the shaman was intoxicated, chanting, communicating with the animals. The shaman exemplifies a more archaic style of being; he's not social. He is rather nearly an animal himself.

RA: A vestige.

TM: A vestige. And a go-between not only in the world of human beings and souls and dreamers, but also between the human world and the animal world.

RS: This was certainly true of the only shaman that I've actually ever stayed with in the Saora tribe in Orissa, India. The village was down in the valley, but he lived at the top of a cliff, where the jungle began. He was often out in the forest trapping animals or just observing them. He lived on the edge; beyond him was the jungle, below him was the village. He was literally at the margin between the two.

TM: This phenomenon of animal-human interaction is bound to have deep archaic roots. I'm very interested in it as part and parcel of the archaic revival.

Truth is a very complicated concept and why shouldn't it be? It's motivated thinkers since thinking began. And, as yet, we have no certain index for it.

CHAPTER 8

SKEPTICISM

*T*erence McKenna: I thought it would be interesting to discuss the whole question of skepticism, and what I call the Balkanization of epistemology, because I think it's an issue that more and more people are becoming aware of. What I mean is this. Somehow, as a part of the agenda of political correctness, it has become not entirely acceptable to criticize, demand substantial evidence, or expect people to make what used to be called old-fashioned sense when they are advancing their speculations. I think this tolerance of unanchored thought and speculation is confusing the evolutionary progress of discourse.

I'm also aware that if you draw the parameters too tight, the baby goes out with the bath water—you become a defender of Scientism or some kind of orthodoxy. So, in my own situation, I've been trying to both understand what is strong, and to be supported in science, and what needs to be criticized. Equally, I've been looking at the alternatives to science—the counterculture, the New Age—and I ask myself, what is strong? What serves the evolution of discourse, and what is, in fact, this type of unanchored thinking that I'm concerned about?

First let me talk a little bit about how I see science. If any one of us were to take what is called a hard scientific approach to many of the phenomena that interest us—which we know exist, and we find rich in implications—they would simply not be allowed as objects of discourse. Psychic pets, the source of the content of the psychedelic experience, and other interesting phenomena would be ruled out of order. So, on one level, there's something wrong with science—or what's called empiricism, skepticism, and positivism. It has different names.

On the other hand, we also run into trouble if we go to the other end of the spectrum and are willing to admit the testimony of iridologists, crop circle enthusiasts, victims of alien abductions, those who channel Atlantis, those who believe vast alien archaeology dots the plains of Mars, and those who claim that pro bono proctologists from distant star systems are making unscheduled house calls. I'm sure that both of you realize that medical professionals, regardless of their species or star system of origin, do not make house calls anymore.

So then, I see this problem. Science is too tight-fisted. It misses much of what is interesting. But to abandon the approach of science is to be without a rudder in an ocean of strident claims and counter claims, many of which are preposterous and certainly not all of which can be true. So, I've been thinking about this for a while. My approach has been to say, well, science went from superstition to its present positivist position through a process of evolution and temporal unfolding. So, using a method I've advocated in other situations, I conducted the following exercise. I said I would move backward through the epistemological history of science to the last sane moment science knew and then analyze what that consists of. I haven't completed this process, but what I find is that a curious betrayal has occurred in science. With the rise of capitalism and industrialism, science has actually allowed assumptions to be made that betrayed its original intent.

What I mean by that is this. Modern science relies on the statistical analysis of data. Measure ten times, add the values, divide by ten, and this tells you how much rain is falling, or how much voltage is flowing through a wire. Something like that. This approach to phenomena inevitably militates against unusual phenomena, because they are statistically insignificant. That's the phrase that is actually used. I think you see my implication. The method of statistical analysis has produced general formalizations of nature's mechanisms, and wonderful products that can be sold and patented, but it's a coarse-veined view of nature. What it militates against seeing are the very things that feed the progress of science—the unassimilated phenomena, the unusual data, the peculiar results of experiments.

So looking at that, I then said, where are we in the history of science? Where did this happen and how was it before? You may wish to correct me a hundred years either way, but I'm very interested in bringing back and appreciate William of Ockham. Aside from the nice things I'm saying about him here, he also had a notion of what he called "unlimited progress" that hasn't been much appreciated. He comes very close to novelty theory belief, that the universe progresses into a merging with the nature of God. But the thing about Ockham that bears on all this is, of course, his famous razor. Although it's been interpreted many ways, this simply says that hypotheses should not be multiplied without necessity. Or, to put it more simply, the simplest explanation of any phenomena should be preferred until found inadequate. Explanations should not be complexified beyond the demands of the problem against which it's being brought to bear.

If we abandon the statistical analysis of nature, we will probably realize that the assumption of temporal invariance about the underlying fields of nature is, in fact, just that—a cheerful assumption, untested and unproved. So, in my hypothetical reformation of epistemological dialogue, we should get rid of statistical analysis. We should dial science back to the late medieval period of Ockham, and we should leave science that way. By applying Ockham's razor we're quickly able to cut away the underbrush that the peripheral and alternative people have brought to the table. Some of it's good, such as things like hypnotism, acupuncture, nutrition therapy, rational approaches to telepathy, and clairvoyance. I don't have a problem with any of this, or with people proposing new models of nature.

What I have a problem with is unanchored, eccentric revelations taking their place at the table— channelings from the Pleiadians, the Sitchinite reconstruction of Ancient Near Eastern archaeology, and the Arguellian distortion of the Mayan accomplishment. I find these things pernicious and easily dealt with if we use Ockham's razor. But when we go too far into the statistical analysis of nature, then we begin to cut away at our own beliefs and assumptions about nature. This threatens Rupert's Morphic Field Theory, my Novelty Theory, and there must be some aspect of all this that would threaten Ralph, if extremely empiricist and positivist criteria were brought to bear. In other words, we've all been called soft in our time. But, in fact, I think our softness indicates a failure of science.

Science has whored itself to the marketplace, and to technology, and interesting high order phenomena like societies, economic crashes, and complex system behavior are going to remain forever blurred in our understanding as long as we rely on statistical analysis. It's a tool that had its place, but to hold onto it indefinitely is going to retard mathematics' ability to give a deeper account of nature. A perfect example of this would be the enshrinement of the so-called uncertainty principle in physics throughout the twentieth century, and the supposed great bridge between science and mysticism. It turns out that's malarkey.

There is no uncertainty principle. David Bohm's formulation of quantum physics gives perfect knowledge of velocity and position without ambiguity. It calls forth the notion of nonlocality. That's why the Heisenburg formulation was preferred. But again, once nonlocality is accepted, some of the things we're interested in are permitted—telepathy, information from other worlds arriving by the morphogenetic field, and so on. Maybe I haven't been as rabble-rousing as expected, by naming in term various heresies to be consigned to the flames, but I do think there are too many loose heads in our canoe, and that no revolution of human thought, that I am aware of, succeeded through uncritical speculation.

Rupert Sheldrake: I think that we have to see the regional problem here—that skepticism or Ockhamism are carrying different social balances in different parts of the world. You live in Hawaii, and Ralph lives in Santa Cruz, California. There's a level of weirdness among some of the theories people have in these areas. Most of the phenomena you've named are typical of Hawaii and California. When you live in England, things take on a rather different perspective. There's a general level of popular skepticism. The general tone of an English pub is one of skepticism.

TM: But aren't crop circles and Graham Hancock all home-grown British phenomena?

RS: They are. But in any pub where they are discussed, every one of them would always have skeptics in the discussion. You're never going to have a kind of thing where you have all believers, except in small crank societies of true believers, which exist. But the general cultural tone is one of skepticism. So the need for a great deal more skepticism doesn't feel quite so urgent if you live in London as it does in Hawaii or California.

Secondly, I think that the skepticism of science that you talk about is a serious threat, and I think that's done more than anything to drive science in a dogmatic direction. It's this kind of skepticism that rules out "paranormal" phenomena at any cost, and feels it has to deny telepathy and other aspects of the sixth sense. According to this perspective, if nonlocality appears to happen, it's just the peculiarity of the details of quantum theory.

TM: Statistical anomaly gets rid of all problems.

RS: Yes. But there are plenty of dogmatic skeptics, like the devotees of the Skeptical Inquirer. That kind of skepticism has done a great deal to force science into this narrow mind-edness. Common sense of the type found in British pubs, and probably in most parts of the United States, would deal quite satisfactorily with the pro bono proctologists from outer space. Anyone who claimed they had had an unscheduled house call would be the butt of a great deal of humor within moments.

TM: No pun intended. But you're right. There is a political problem. Though the British have this reputation in America for being the epitome of politeness, actually, in a British pub, people are willing to blow the whistle on what they perceive as absurdity.

RS: By jokes and through humor.

TM: The New Age is utterly humorless. The reigning paradigm of political correctness demands that you treat all of these testimonies and bits of news with complete equanimity. It's thought to be rather out of sorts to suggest that anybody shouldn't be taken seriously. The belief is that truth can't be known, so all there is is opinions. You speak from your knowledge of calculus and world history, and this person speaks from the latest transmission from fallen Atlantis—and this is all placed on an equal footing. It's crazy making, and it also guarantees that trivialness is the entire enterprise. I mean, I just don't think fluff heads can make any revolution in human history.

Ralph Abraham: In order to understand what you're saying, I have to really try to figure out what a fluff head is. This is the crux. I like your historical approach. As we agree that science is rather in a bad place now, we can look back, find where it went wrong, go back there, and start over again. This is actually what fundamentalists do. Our ethics are gone, so we're going to go back to something like the first speeches of Mohammed. I feel uncomfortable with William of Ockham's idea of simplicity. The modern form is probably Kolmogorov's measure of complexity. This determines what the length and bytes of the smallest computer program would be that could approximate this data set within epsilon.

The problem with this, technically speaking, is that this year's technology would give a much smaller measure than last year's technology, because we've learned new tricks for building models. Or it may only depend upon the computer language that more or less was used to build the model. So, in other words, there is no simple measure of simplicity. Given three explanations, we're not sure what is the simplest one. There's no mathematics that could really be applied. It becomes a subjective judgment. Therefore, I think that you've suggested a one-dimensional scale of fluff-head—the McKenna fluff scale—where, down at one end we have what even Wolpert thinks is okay. Over at the other end we have the test that can be applied to Pleiadians to see if they're real or not.

So this scale is marked by two points. There's the point at which you think that to the right of it it's too fluffy, and to the left it's okay. Then there's another point where science agrees it's okay. By doing this you're ruling some things out and accepting other things. But Wolpert says morphogenetic fields are not okay, and DNA is. So there are these two points that you've described as being on some linear scale of fluff. I think you'd like this fluff scale in order to appeal to mathematics, and to some kind of real science—if there is such a thing—so that it can redirect our focus when the religion of science has gotten off track. But this is what bothers me. I wish that this were true, but I'd have no faith in it—that somewhere in the sky, or in the deepest bowels of the earth, there is a measuring stick which can somehow measure the truth of something, even if it's just a degree of truth. In chaos logic, you don't have true and false. You have truth as a percentage between zero and a hundred percent. Chaos logic would be a good alternative for you.

The truth of a proposition—using a formal logic, like Zeno's paradox—is only a temporal assessment. The input of the measuring stick of truth lasts only until we get another measurement. So what we know so far is sixty-percent true. Now we assume that at sixty percent true that's the input to another assessment. Then we find it's sixty-six percent true. When we've got the input of another assessment, then it's sixty-four percent true. Hopefully, this process of successive judgment, which could be regarded as the history of science—from the past through William of Ockham, on through the infinite future—would converge or something. But in chaotic logic it doesn't converge, because certain kinds of propositions, like Zeno's paradox, are circular in a way. In circling around they have chaotic attractors always giving different results.

It never settles down. It gives changing estimates between zero and a hundred percent. From this perspective—the successor of Aristotelian logic, which served science up until around 1985—you can't have a clear measuring stick of truth or a clear scale of fluff. So the attempt to make something perfectly clear might be doomed to failure. We understand it, then, as something psychological. I'm applying Ludwig Fleck here. Fleck is the founder of the sociology of science, which does a Freudian analysis of the scientific community.

As parents in the sixties, we were very libertine with our children. Now we see these children have gone on, and they're having children. They're much stricter, and there's the idea that in successive generations people are more or less strict with their children. I think they're more or less strict about fluff also. So the fluff scale is actually a sociological aspect of a given culture or civilization which fluctuates wildly in time. I think that as we age and as we receive input from young people—as far as the morphogenetic sequence of a fluff scale is concerned—we're affected by them. We're becoming a little more critical. We've become more critical of ourselves, because a decade ago we were more open. So our fluff scale is changing, and, therefore, we have to rearrange our social grid. Some people that were previously okay are now too fluffy for us, or their brains have fallen out.

TM: I think I agree with almost everything you said. On the end of pointing out that truth is a very difficult thing to assess, you didn't mention Kurt Gödel. Certainly his proof that no formal system produces all true statements shows that even ordinary arithmetic is subject to debate and represents a kind of circularity. So, on one end, I completely agree with you that truth is a very complicated concept and why shouldn't it be? It's motivated thinkers since thinking began. And, as yet, we have no certain index for it.

You mentioned that you thought my approach was one-dimensional, and I agree from your example. But much of your criticism was couched in the vocabulary of symbolic logic and analytical deconstruction. Here's a way we might go at this. Agreeing that it's a messy problem, let's also agree that the solutions may be somewhat messy. So, for instance, perhaps we need to talk about kinds of fluff. I immediately identify two kinds of fluff. One is unscientific speculation, persistent throughout history, and with the consistent provenance.

RS: Are you referring to religion or mythology?

TM: I wasn't going to attack religion. I was thinking of more marginal ideas, but religion is a good example. I was going to suggest alchemy. Alchemy believes certain things about matter which science absolutely abhors and rejects. The history of Alchemy is far older than the history of science. It has always been in existence, and its thinkers have always evolved their field of concern. So that's one kind of fluff-fluff with punch, because it has historical continuity. But what are we to make of someone who produces a complete cosmological model generated in the past ten years by themselves alone. They never read Plato. They know no mathematics. They never read the Bible.

They just got it all in one download. It's a faith that tells you that vegetables lose their auric fields unless peeled with wooden implements, that major earth changes have already happened but are invisible to most people, that there are only one hundred real people alive on the planet anyway—everyone else is a simulacrum from a different dimension. In other words, preposterous on the face of it—history-less, idiosyncratic, and utterly unanchored to any body of previous human thought, sanctioned or unsanctioned.

RS: So the question before us is, how do we distinguish all these speculations from one that superficially might appear to be similar— the revelations summarized in your book *The In-*

visible Landscape? How do we distinguish between your book and all the rest?

TM: I think the category of *The Invisible Landscape* is *I Ching* commentary. The *I Ching* is a legitimate object of speculative discourse. It has been since pre-Han times.

RA: Okay, so let's say we accept a two-dimensional model for fluff—where there's deepest fluff, like *I Ching* commentaries, and more superficial fluff, like the entire manifest universe is the circulation of a single electron.

What is it that science hates besides Rupert? Science hates homeopathy, acupuncture, and alternative medicine altogether. Science hates cold fusion. So a lot of things would be missed. This makes me think of those paradigm shifts that redirected the path of science. For example, the discovery of continental drift or the Ice Ages. The discovery of the Ice Ages was a really terrific discovery by some mountain climbers, and it was rejected by science for thirty or forty years. It is one of the few successful examples of a paradigm shift in science.

TM: You mentioned thirty or forty years. I think one way to think about this problem is to give the school of fluff a certain amount of time to advance their agenda. But if, after twenty, thirty, forty years they go nowhere, they should lose their place in the discourse or move to the back of the room. I think this should be applied to science as well. For example, science has been beating its breast since 1950 about how they were about to elucidate the mechanism of memory. I think it's time to just pull the plug on that. You've had fifty years to flail at this with every tool available, and you have zilch to show for it. Similarly, the people who believe aliens from other star systems are visiting this planet—with great plans for mankind—have been running that riff since 1947. It's time for them to lower their voices and let other people have something to say.

RA: I'd say maybe a century or two. Why are you so tight?

TM: Because they inhibit progress. Other fields have created multiple revolutions in the same time scale.

RA: But sometimes progress is very subtle. For example, they didn't find any memory mechanisms in the brain, but, while they were looking, they did figure out how to do a certain kind of surgery that helps with the removal of tumors.

TM: I would challenge you to make a list of spin-off effects from the New Age that would reduce the suffering of mankind. There have been a few back-scratchers, some nutritional supplements, and a mantra or two, but in terms of the money consumed, the lives distorted, the hype that we've all had to put up with, there has been little of value.

RA: Okay, if we were the National Science Foundation, and we've been funding channelers for years in the hope that they would find gold in South America, then we might withdraw our funding at this point. But we can't make it illegal for them to channel.

TM: No. What we have to legitimize is critical discussion, so that when someone stands up, and starts talking about the face on Mars, people behave as they apparently behave in

British pubs. People just stand up and say "Malarkey, mate!" and force people to experience a critical deconstruction of their ideas. The face on Mars is a perfect example. The Voyager sends a low-resolution image of what might be a face, and all of these self-promoting, so-called ex-NASA scientists gather around, and proclaim this thing an alien artifact. When I hear the phrase "ex-NASA scientist" in the New Age, I reach for my revolver.

When the first Mars orbiter fails at orbital injection around Mars, they scream "Conspiracy! Mankind isn't ready for the truth." Eighteen months later the second Martian orbiter goes into orbit flawlessly. NASA, responding to the previous hullabaloo, actually moves this site up in its photographic agenda—exactly under the conditions these people say it must be photographed under. It's clearly an eroded mesa, part of the Martian landscape, no different from any other. Immediately the face on Mars's people scream that the data has been tampered with, that all kinds of terrible things have gone wrong. One guy sent me email saying, "if there isn't a face on Mars, there will be in the future." Someone else wrote me and said, "obviously the aliens wouldn't leave an artifact. The face on Mars is cleverly disguised as an eroded mesa."

RA: I agree. But I'm not sure that it's good to rant against the face on Mars, because there's no way, by William of Ockham or whatever, that you could have ruled out the possibility that there was really a pocket watch on Mars. In fact, they do know there's life here and there. There's water on the Moon. There's not a face on Mars, but there's something that nobody suspected that was found by going there. So my fear is that by drawing the line too tight, many discoveries will be missed. I think that a certain amount of open-mindedness is necessary for novelty to come in and to nourish the evolution of the collective mind.

RS: I've got a political answer to this. However much we choose to define the criteria, we have no power whatever to enforce them—unless we run a funding committee like the National Science Foundation or the British Medical Research Council, or unless we are the editors of a prominent journal such as *Nature* or *Science*. Under those conditions—through controlling grants or the editorial policies of major journals— you really do shape and influence the science community. But the people in those positions are unlikely to listen to what we say. So the realistic question is, how could the system be reformed?

One proposal is advanced in the book *The Economic Laws of Scientific Research*, by a Cambridge biochemist named Terence Kealey. He shows that in the nineteenth century, when there was a great deal of creativity and originality in both Britain and America, there was a great diversity of sources of funding. There was very little public money. The funding came from wealthy individuals and from companies that needed to do the science in order to make what they needed.

By contrast, by the late nineteenth century, continental science was highly professionalized and institutionalized. In Britain and America, it was not until after the Second World War that science became so centralized and state controlled. People like Vannevar Bush got the idea of a military-industrial complex—with big science, and massive government funding, especially for military research. In Britain, we also have a centralized system of science funding through government research councils, which decide who gets the grants. These councils are run by small committees of establishment scientists and representatives of large corporations. This imposes a kind of monopoly control, and uniformity of thought—the enemy of unorthodox thinking.

Because Kealey is a believer in free markets, he suggests that the only answer to this is not to follow Sir Francis Bacon's idea of central government spending, where you have a sort of state priesthood of scientists. Instead, Kealey advocates reduced central government spending. Science would then be paid for in accordance with any interest group that's got enough lobbying power. For example, there are a large number of people who want organic food who could lobby for money to be spent on organic farming research, which at present gets very little funding.

If priorities were set by popular opinion, pet research would be high on the biological agenda, not the sequencing of more proteins, or the cloning of more genes to help the biotechnology industry. But instead, pet research isn't even on the agenda set by the small elite, who have no interest in the interests of ordinary people. But it's the ordinary people who in fact provide the money for all government research through their taxes.

RA: I agree that the monopolistic control of financing scientific research worldwide is bad. Nevertheless, the National Science Foundation does rely on the judgment of peer reviewers and a group of experts. Finally, it's their opinions that direct the flow of money. That would also be true if there was no central control, and you had every industry financing its own research. Actually, that's the way it works in the pet food industry. There are two or three pet food companies that are outstanding for their research on the dietary needs of cats and dogs, and they do research based on funds that are coming in from pet owners. This is the nineteenth century model. So it still exists to a degree.

RS: As well as introducing more democratic principles into science funding, I think we need to extend skepticism to the sciences themselves. There's an interesting paper in the recent issue of the Journal of the History of Medicine on the history of double-blind techniques. Double-blind techniques were invented by Benjamin Franklin in Paris in the late eighteenth century when he was appointed by King Louis XVI to head up a Royal Commission to investigate the claims of Anton Mesmer, as the whole of Europe was talking about Mesmerism and animal magnetism.

Franklin and the other members of the Royal Commission were firmly of the opinion that this was some kind of delusion, a product of people's minds and their beliefs. In order to test this hypothesis, they developed blind methodologies where people didn't know who was being treated and who wasn't. The blind methodologies literally involved blindfolding people to find out if they could still detect this animal magnetism. Often they couldn't.

Blind techniques became a standard practice when skeptics examined marginal phenomena like hypnotism and the claims of homeopaths. The homeopaths took this criticism seriously, and they were the first group in scientific research to internalize blind techniques by running their own blind trials. It wasn't until after the Second World War that the standard randomized double-blind clinical trial became the norm in medical research, and it didn't really become widespread until the 1950s or 1960s. So this is another case of blind techniques being internalized. In parapsychology, blind techniques were internalized as early as the 1880s and in regular psychology in the 1960s, with the recognition of experimenter effects.

I recently carried out a survey of the use of blind techniques in different branches of science by analyzing the "Methods" section of papers published in leading journals. In this survey, which I summarized in the Skeptical Inquirer, I found that the use of blind techniques has gone furthest in parapsychology, where 85 percent of published experiments were carried out blind. In medicine and psychology, where everyone pays lip service to the idea of blind techniques, in practice the number of blind or double-blind papers was below 20 percent. In biology, the number of blind papers, out of over 900 reviewed, was less than 1 percent, and in the physical sciences—chemistry and physics—the number of blind studies was zero. We then interviewed top professors in leading departments of physics, chemistry, biology, and molecular biology at Cambridge, Oxford, and other universities. Most people in the physics and chemistry departments there neither use nor teach blind techniques.

The idea that modern science is so objective and unbiased in these areas seems to be based on the notion that, by putting on a white coat, one becomes completely objective, and is not subject to the biases that everybody is. So I suggest checking out blind techniques in the laboratory. Do you get different results in a physics experiment if you do it blind compared with doing it with the usual open conditions, where you know which sample is which?

TM: The New Age could probably profit from this as well. It would probably wipe out most of the things I'm objecting to.

RA: The popularity of double-blind methodology in parapsychology is obviously due to the difficulty researchers have convincing people of the validity of the results. In other words, it's due to the special weight of skepticism that's applied to the fringe of speculation. So, somehow, there's the fundamental dialectic of the evolutionary mind. It has to do with the balance and interplay between speculation and skepticism. These are the two forces at work, and we want them to both be healthy and freely interplay. If a new technique such as double-blind experiment can work, then the interplay of these forces will guarantee that it's used. To summarize your case against the New Age fuzz, Terence, there seems to be an area in the evolving mind where the speculation is not balanced by an appropriate amount of skepticism. You want to shine a flashlight of skeptical consideration onto that area of unbalanced fuzz. We're interested in balanced fuzz.

TM: Speculation and skepticism begin to sound like novelty and habit. So maybe these things are just counter-flows in the intellectual life of the culture that redress each other, and though we do have certain long-running forms of fuzz, it does tend to correct itself over time. But in the present historical moment, we are seeing an incredible fragmentation, syncretic theorizing, and a richness of ideological competition due shortly to self-correct.

RS: But what I see on the fringes is a whole lot of small cults and gurus that are all vying for space in *Common Ground* magazine. It's a highly competitive market. What's keeping all of them in check is competition. If one cult does particularly well, it grows. Others fade away if they don't get enough supporters. There's a free market with a clamor of competing claims.

That's on the fringes. But the main ground is occupied by a kind of Stalinist central control of government-funded official science, which marginalizes everything else. A free market approach would allow a more informed debate.

TM: I'm a little surprised, because you seem to be implying that here is yet another area where the solution to all problems is the practice of untrammeled capitalism, and the unleashing of unrestrained market forces. Welcome to the new millennium.

RA: It's almost the definition of science that it's to be an alternative to the diversity that has been experienced in world cultural history in the sphere of religion. Very early on people knew that every town had different gods. This multiplicity was acceptable. Even though some people thought their gods were more powerful than the gods of other ones, they agreed that there would be a lot of gods. So everything fit together in a context of diversity.

Science appealed to people who lost faith in religion. In science they hoped that there could be a unique global planetary system of thought. Many people would think it appropriate that there's a monopolistic control of the funding of scientific research, because each thing is supposedly going to reinforce, validate, and confirm everything else—because this is the idea of scientific truth.

I think the idea of a free market in science would require giving up the idea that there is some kind of absolute scientific truth, and that a given question could be settled either true or false according to this universal canon. I don't believe in this idea. That's why a free market in scientific research would be good. Perhaps if science was liberalized in this way, it would become very much like religion, where you would have groups like Baptists, Vendantists and Shiites who would believe in this or that system. You have to wonder if this kind of diversity would be acceptable by our species in the future or not, and what's the alternative.

Boundaries which are too firm (iron curtains) may be involved in world problems, and could be treated with therapies informed by the new math. Chaos and cosmos must be properly balanced for a healthy social system.

Perhaps, as there's an increase of complexity in our culture, as we approach the Eschaton, there's an accompanying decrease as fractality actually vanishes at an alarming rate. This is what's meant by "the death of nature."

CHAPTER 9

FRACTALS

Ralph Abraham: This epic in four parts I'll call "Fractals on My Mind."

Part one: The sandy beach.

If we look at a map of the Hawaiian Islands, we find a firm curve between Hawaii and the Pacific Ocean. But if we go down to the shore, we find a sandy beach. It is the boundary between land and sea, but it is not a firm curve. There is water in the sand, and sand in the water. The more closely we look at the beach, the more indistinction we see. The transition from land to sea is a fractal. It is spatially chaotic. It is *natural*. The Milky Way is a sandy beach in the sky. It is *natural* also. Nature teaches us fractal geometry and chaos theory.

Part two: Two roads diverged in a yellow wood.

Dynamical systems have attractors and basins. Imagine a dynamical system with two attractors, red and green. No matter where you begin, you will be attracted to one attractor or the other. Perform an experiment by choosing a starting position, then following the rules of the system, to find which attractor is your destiny. Color the starting position red or green, depending on the outcome. After a million experiments starting from different positions, the domain is mostly colored red and green. The red region is called the basin of attraction of the red attractor, likewise with the green basin. The domain, colored red and green in this way, is called the basin portrait of the system. Between the red and the green are the basin boundaries, which might be outlined in yellow. The yellow boundaries, in a generic dynamical system, are fractals: a wide, frothy zone, of mixed red and green, like a sandy beach. Or a yellow wood.

Part three: Fractals in my mind.

Both of the two little math lessons I just completed are applicable to psychology. Let's imagine, as Kurt Lewin might, that a person's mind has its own space. Lewin was the founder of social psychology, and within that the notion of field theory in psychology. The field operated in a mental space, which he called the life space. The mental process was, to him, a dynamical system (the field) working in the life space. Thus, we may regard the multiple attractors and basins of the psychological field as the stable states of the mind. I am suggesting that in a normal psyche, the basin boundaries are thick fractals, which permit a kind of porosity between these components of the psyche, and thus, integration. But in another mind, the basin boundaries may be like concrete walls or iron curtains. This is a dynamical model for multiple personality syndrome: the sandy beach model. From the perspective of this model, the pathology comes from the poverty of chaos in the basin boundaries, and thus I call it *MPD*, for multiple personality dischaos. If we were therapists, we could try to devise a treatment to increase the fractal dimension of basin boundaries, based on chaos theory and fractal geometry, which are new branches of post-Euclidean math.

Part four: Fractals in the collective mind.

Rather than going on with individual psychology here, I want to look at the mind of the whole enchilada from this point of view. The collective conscious and unconscious of our society is a massively complex system, which Kurt Lewin also described in the paradigm of life fields. Chaos theory suggests a sandy beach model for this massive system also. Thus, boundaries which are too firm (iron curtains) may be involved in world problems, and could be treated with therapies informed by the new math. Chaos and cosmos must be properly balanced for a healthy social system.

Rupert Sheldrake: I'd like to try and summarize, Ralph, what you said, and see if I can add to it.

Personalities—and of course social relationships and international relations and the behavior of different groups of pigeons—fall into different basins, and we can visualize this as a landscape containing different valleys. If something's in a particular region, the ball will roll down in a particular valley.

Each of these basins represents a different kind of subpersonality. You pointed out that personalities are made up of different sub-personalities, which is currently a very fashionable view. Everyone's talking about subpersonalities. For example, the Jungian psychologist James Hillman says we need a polytheistic psychology, where all the different gods and goddesses not only represent the archetypes, but they are real in some sense; we're possessed by different ones at different times. We're not a single personality with different functions, but a kind of emulsion of a number of different personalities. Everywhere we find these multiple models, of which yours is one. All of them seem to be saying that we must get away from monotheism, which is reflected in psychology by the idea of the central, dominating ego. We've got to build more democratic models where you have a kind of grassroots democracy, with all these different personalities.

A second point you seem to be making is that the boundary between these different basins is not a straight line or a rigid wall but rather a fractal boundary, namely one that has many ins and outs and curves and filigrees and patterns. With that kind of boundary, moving from one basin to another is very easy because you never quite know where you are and can cross boundaries without realizing it, whereas a rigid wall makes it difficult to get from one to the other.

I'd like to take up the idea of the plurality of models. Terence's model is monotheistic, in that he has a single *Eschaton*, and this takes us immediately to the polytheism versus monotheism argument. My view of polytheism is that in all its actual existing forms, it is not in fact radical polytheism. It involves a plurality with some overarching unity beyond it. My question to you is, are you advocating a radical polytheism, and denying an overarching unity?

RA: No. My main message has to do with the rigidity of boundaries in between things. I think that everybody would agree that there is plurality in religion, in life, in the mind, in the stream, in the sky, and so on. What's important is the rigidity of the boundaries in between these things. If you worship in the Shiva temple is it okay to go to the Rama temple?

Do you have to be faithful to one god and never admit the existence of others? This is a denial of something that's obvious even to children, and it inevitably brings about a disintegration of the personality.

In this religious or mythological context it's appropriate to think of Shiva and concepts of that sort as attractors. There are multiple attractors. Considering the population of the planet through all times, there are zillions of attractors, and some people have visited one and other people have visited two or three and so on. An openness to all attractors, I guess I would say, is some kind of prerequisite for the stability and longevity of a culture, or the health of an individual. This idea is based on a cosmology in which the stream has the same morphology as the heavens, which have the same morphology as some abstract mathematical object. Under the ambience of this idea, our experience of nature is that rigid walls are very unstable.

RS: They're not that unstable. Our own skin, for example, has pores in it and is not absolutely smooth. Nevertheless, it forms a clear functional boundary, and everywhere you look in biology you find functional boundaries. There's a cell membrane around each cell. It's not an infinitely permeable boundary.

RA: It has little holes in it with pumps that are designed for particular things in the environment. The permeability is, as it were, part of a structure that's rigidly connected with that species. If these holes were plugged up then of course the cell would instantly die.

RS: Of course, you're not denying the importance of boundaries. Your whole model is based on boundaries, isn't it?

RA: That's right. It has to do with their crookedness.

RS: Their crookedness is the mathematical model for their permeability.

RA: Yes.

Terence McKenna: It seems extraordinarily arcane. Nature is fractal. This is a new discovery, and it's a very powerful insight, but it doesn't wipe out some of our previous accomplishments; I'm thinking of all the work that was done to show that these systems are also hierarchical. Without tossing the baby out with the bath water, it might be better to say it's fractal and hierarchical. We're back to Whitehead's notion of certain stubborn facts that are, I suppose, like raisins of resistance embedded in this fractal ocean of infinite permeability. I think above all these psychoboundaries and membranes there is ultimately a frame that is all-inclusive and defined. The form of monotheism I've probably fallen under the sway of, is some kind of neoplatonic pyramid of ever-ascending abstract hypostases that leads into the One. If what we mean by the *Eschaton* is the absence of boundaries, then what we're saying is that the fractalization of reality occurs ultimately on such fine scales that from the point of view of the perceiver, the boundaries have dissolved completely. Or the boundary and the thing bound have become so homogenized that it no longer makes sense to speak of boundary and medium. I picture it as a kind of extremely marbleized liquid or surface where every domain can be found to be lying next to a mutually exclusive other domain, rather like the kinds of diagrams you get when you carry out four-color mapping problems to fourth and fifth stages of resolution. You have these extraordinarily complicated structures where every point lies next to the boundary that separates it from points that have been somehow defined as other. I'm not sure that we have any disagreement here.

RA: What we've got here in your description is a speculation built upon a speculation built upon a speculation and coming eventually from some kind of absolute and pure faith. The One, to Plotinus, was something that you could explore toward, but not actually arrive at. We have to understand, on the testimony of these early experts, that The One is an article of faith, and even the best traveling shaman has only been so far. The assumption of the existence of The One, beyond this, is monotheism at its best. God is called "The One" to make sure that you don't think perhaps it's Two. I agree with your idea that cosmos is hierarchical. I don't even care if it has a finite number of layers or an infinite number. However, the wildest shaman has traveled and seen only another image, maybe more complex, of what we see in ordinary reality and nature. There are multiple basins, there are fractal boundaries, there are many possibilities, different regions, complexity, where harmony is hierarchically organized, and we've never gotten to the top. Therefore, to say it's one or two or three can only be an article of faith, not an extrapolation from observation, normal or arcane. We're talking about pure faith. When you get to the top frame, I don't see any reason why it shouldn't have two basins, separated by a fractal.

TM: My understanding of fractals is that they are a kind of homogenization of levels not present, domains distant, and that the idea is if you have a sufficient sample of the fractal, not very large, you can in fact extrapolate the contours of the entire system. Therefore it isn't necessary to send the shaman or mathematician for a total overview. The cosmological principle can be extrapolated from local measurement and local physics.

RA: Without an article of faith, you can't get a cosmological principle. We don't have any evidence from the boundaries of space.

TM: Isn't the idea that fractals are a kind of holographic plan that recurs on many levels, always following the same pattern? If you have ten levels and you know the pattern on 2 through 7, you also know the pattern on 1, 8, 9 and 10.

RA: Few fractals in nature have that property, which is a special property of self-similar fractals that are like integers within the field of all real numbers. They are exceptional. Mostly it just means you have two basins, red and green, and their boundary is kind of stirred up so wherever you are you're within one millimeter of each side, or even a tenth of a millimeter of each side.

TM: Well, I've limited my model building to the use of self-similar fractals. My model of the *Eschaton*, at least on a mathematical level, is self-similar.

RA: If you have three basins fractally entwined, then wherever you are in the sandy beach, you're not only within one millimeter of the red and green, but the yellow one is there also. That means, if you travel as a shaman and you see this pattern at the end of time, and there's any blur in your vision, anything slightly human remaining in your travel, you might see it as one, even though it isn't. You would mistakenly see it as a blur of the three colors into a kind of gray *Eschaton*.

RS: In some circles this is known as the mystery of the Holy Trinity. Theological attempts to deal with this problem have led to a variety of models where you have the idea that the ultimate is not an undifferentiated unity but rather a pattern of relationships. In the Taoist model you have the Yin and the Yang with a kind of fractal boundary between them. The circle containing the two is the whole that unifies them. In the model of the Holy Trinity, the Father is the source of the Word and the Spirit. The underlying metaphor is speaking. The spirit is the breath on which the word can happen, as you breathe out. The spoken word is a pattern of vibrations and harmonics that's probably some kind of fractal pattern in time. It would be hard to say which is the breath and which are the sounds, and how you can separate the vibration from the sounds. This would seem to be the kind of model, in another form, that you have in mind. The unity comes from the sense of interrelationship and common source.

All these models of an ultimate unity are models of a relationship which something holds together. The hidden agenda behind your fractal model is that although you can't see unity within them, the hidden unity behind it all is the mathematics governing the fractals. For most mathematicians, these mathematical structures exist in some kind of Platonic realm beyond space and time, even if it's only in the imagination of mathematicians. There's some kind of hidden unity containing the diversity, and somehow generating it. I would say the unity is implicit in any mathematical model in the hidden mathematical object behind the manifested pattern.

RA: My point is not so much about the multiplicity or unity. I agree that everything is unified at some level. The point is more about the boundaries. If you have a dynamical system with different basins and they have fractal boundaries then, as a matter of fact, no matter how you perceive it, no matter what experiment you do, you will perceive unity. When you don't perceive unity, it is in the pathological case where you've erected an iron curtain. If you have iron curtains, then unity essentially has been defeated by the disease of dischaos. Therefore, when we see this in nature, in history, in social systems, in ourselves, we have to beware of these iron curtains, because they create an unnecessarily multiple situation.

Here we've expressed a yearning for a peaceful state beyond language. If you practice chanting, meditations and so on, then you are intentionally increasing the fractality of the boundaries, and therefore the integration of the parts into a unity. If unity is your goal, then you have to examine the fractal width of all your boundaries, and guard against boundaries that are too thin.

RS: How do you fractalize your boundaries? Can you give a personal example?

RA: In the emerging science of neural nets this is called annealing. One thing you can do is take a psychedelic. Another thing you can do is go to a culture that's really different from your own and stay there for seven years on a farm or something. If you have a mate of any gender, you're certainly in a more chaotic situation. These two-person units definitely have diseases, and few of them survive these days. I'm making a suggestion here as to what's the trouble, and I'm suggesting a strategy, a kind of a therapeutic technique. People are trying out this idea, by the way, for therapy in relationships.

RS: Can you give an example of how the fractalization of boundaries would work therapeutically in a relationship?

RA: First of all there's a diagnostic phase, in which the therapist is trained in chaos theory instead of Freudian theory. When a boundary has been detected with a pathologically low dimension or thickness, a therapy is devised especially for it, consisting of some carefully safeguarded experiments in violating the boundary, or mixing boundaries. One common strategy involves play in a sandbox. You've seen this. The therapist's office has all these toys that return the client to preverbal mode of expression. I'm not a therapist, but I think an advancing theory is helpful in devising therapies.

In the United States people are getting together in small groups for self-therapy, because they feel that a therapist not having multiple personality dischaos has no idea really what's going on. These groups studying chaos theory have devised a kind of therapeutic psychodrama, which they write, direct, and perform in public, in cities around the United States. There's a network of these that base their approach on my paper on multiple personality dischaos. I can give you a report next year on how these experiments work out. Some therapists believe that they may be fatal and that I should be imprisoned, but the patients themselves are very enthusiastic. They're really having a wonderful time. Depression is a really serious condition. If a therapy was devised that cured bipolar personality dischaos without drugs, a lot of people would be helped.

TM: Given what you've said about the goals of this therapy, wouldn't it just be simpler to give these people psychedelics?

RA: I've personally had good results with psychedelics, but I'm not sure everyone would. It would be nice if we had several alternative strategies, some of which could be done on a Sunday evening, where you still feel okay about going to work on Monday morning. Like vitamin pills.

TM: Since you've had such good luck with psychedelics, why are you so reluctant to advocate it?

RA: I have been advocating, or at least if not advocating, confessing in public that for me there have been very good results with psychedelics. I've quite recently had a certain amount of hostile mail and telephone calls; even people coming to the university to hasten my demise. They seem to think that psychedelics are drugs. There's also the aspect of legality, where many people are in jail with 20, 30 and 40-year jail sentences. I think that the atmosphere of paranoia in the world today might even make psychedelics much less effective as medicine for dischaos.

TM: If the paranoia and legal barriers were removed, it sounds like you're advocating something fairly close to what Salvador Roquet's school settled into.

RA: I don't know Salvador Roquet.

TM: He was a much-regarded psychotherapist who worked in Mexico for many years, who treated people and trained therapists with psychedelics. Then he showed them Auschwitz footage and very highly charged emotional material, the idea being to reduce them to an absolutely basic jelly of dissolved boundaries.

RA: It sounds disgusting.

TM: I agree. I'm trying to find out how what you're advocating is different.

RA: It takes only very subtle medicine to decrease rigid walls. Even the very idea of it may be enough, as a matter of fact. That's the therapy idea. Once consciousness is adjusted so that sensitivity to your own process actually observes these things and considers them undesirable, they automatically begin to disappear under the self-created action of one's own psyche. After all, nature is playing a part, and mathematical necessity reveals itself in the Milky Way, the sandy beach, and the human psyche as well. There's a tendency toward help. These diseases of rigid barriers, like other diseases, exist primarily in the rejection of the cure, and the cure can be found within. One has to realize that when people suffer this disease, which is essentially universal, it's inherited from a culture that has the disease itself. The cure consists of identifying the difficulty as essentially a cultural pattern, and then disowning it by becoming more of an expatriate of our own culture. That's why visiting another culture and living there for a few months or years is sometimes enough to liberate people from rigid patterns.

TM: This comes very close to the nineteenth century prescription for most emotional difficulties of a few months at the seashore, in Italy preferably. In both cases you want to establish a new environmental attitude through distance from cultural values, either achieved through journeys with drugs or journeys to foreign lands.

RA: A walk in the woods is perhaps all it takes.

TM: It's a search for perspective, achieved by distancing.

RA: A kind of mathematical perspective. Our culture has suffered this particular disease over a mere span of 6,000 years. That's all we have to recover from.

TM: The particular disease being boundary anxiety?

RA: Patriarchal, monotheistic, hierarchical, misunderstood...

TM: Constipated, linear...

RS: Is there any culture that has managed to avoid dischaos?

RA: I think so, but I don't have direct experience of aboriginal cultures. The culture we live in has by now covered the entire globe, and the exceptions are near to extinction. Anthropologists used to study wild tribes before they were contacted by the civilizations now dominating the entire sphere. Unfortunately, civilization arrived in the form of these anthropologists, and this was the kiss of death for those cultures.

TM: This is a theme near and dear to me. Certainly, in living Amazon cultures, one of the hardest things for a "civilized" person to put up with is the fact that there are no boundaries. Everybody lives in a grand house without walls. Defecation, sexuality, death, domestic hassling, disciplining of children, everything goes on in the presence of everyone else and no one from age 6 to 90 feels any constraint whatsoever about making comments, suggestions, and offering free advice. It's a hard thing to embrace, even with the knowledge that it's going to be good for you.

RA: There are degrees of boundaries. I think the permeability of boundaries is important, and our culture has devoted excess attention to the walled fortress, necessitated by the violence some people would associate with the patriarchy. For whatever reason there's been a necessity of Bauhaus concrete walls around the town, locks on the doors and houses, electronic motion detectors, video cameras at the bank card machine, and so on. Perhaps, as there's an increase of complexity in our culture, as we approach the *Eschaton*, there's an accompanying decrease as fractality actually vanishes at an alarming rate. This is what's meant by "the death of nature."

RS: Ralph, when I last visited your house in Santa Cruz, I noticed a rigid, straight fence dividing your property from your undesirable neighbors, who have motorcycle scrambles on their land and make a terrible noise.

RA: Boys with guns, that's right.

RS: What we need here is a new product, the fractal fence, which would go down very well in California, some kind of fractal boundary, instead of old style posts with barbed wire.

RA: Mazes where people can get lost if they try to pass.

RS: Except that, with the slightest gust of wind or unpredicted chaotic event, these motorcycles would suddenly zoom past your front door.

The actual sky is something of which most people are abysmally ignorant. In most traditional cultures people could recognize the stars. Mariners, shepherds, and ordinary people knew the basic constellations in the sky, and the planets.

CHAPTER 10

THE HEAVENS

Rupert Sheldrake: A recovery of the sense of the life of nature is going on for a variety of reasons in a variety of ways; through the archaic revival, the Gaia hypothesis, deep ecology and the ecology movement in general. As I have shown in my book *The Rebirth of Nature*, science itself is pointing us in the direction of a recovery of the sense of the life of nature. It is, I think, happening all around us.

There's a further step I think we need to take, beyond seeing the natural world as alive, namely seeing it as sacred. In the past the heavens were sacred and so was the earth, especially the sacred places that were the focuses of power, recognized in every land by every culture. They were recognized by American Indians in America, by Europeans, both pre-Christian and Christian, by Australian Aborigines, by Africans, by Jews in the Holy Land. In all cultures people related to this sense of the sacredness of the land and the earth through journeying to places of power, in pilgrimage. Pilgrimage was suppressed for the first time in human history by the Protestant reformers in Northern Europe during the Reformation, creating a void that led to a desacralization of nature. The sense of the sacred became focused entirely on man. Religion was centered on the drama of fall and redemption played out between man and God. Nature had nothing to do with it except as a kind of backdrop, or the means for people enriching themselves, becoming prosperous as a sign of God's grace and providence.

The English couldn't bear this void caused by the suppression of pilgrimage, and within a few generations had invented tourism, which is best seen as a form of secularized pilgrimage. I believe a paradigm shift from tourism back to pilgrimage could go a long way to help resacralize the earth. Another way in which the natural world was sacralized was through seasonal festivals. Not just individuals but the whole community participated in festivals that marked the changing seasons of the earth—the solstices, the equinoxes, and the festivals which the Christian world has inherited from pagan roots such as Christmas and Easter.

What I want to talk about now is resacralizing the heavens, and this involves going considerably further than anyone I know has yet gone.

Before the seventeenth century, when people used the word "heaven," they were referring both to the sky and to the abode of God, the angels and the blessed. Since the seventeenth century the sky has been secularized and the heavens are now considered simply the domain of astronomy. Heaven, the abode of the angels, God and the blessed, is considered some kind of psychological or spiritual state that has nothing whatever to do with the actual sky. Heaven isn't located out there; it's located in our persons in some way, or else in some spiritual realm utterly disconnected from the sky. We've grown so used to this. For example, if you suggest to Christians that when they say "Our Father who art in heaven," that this implies that God is located in the sky, they very rapidly become embarrassed by the suggestion and brush it aside as some kind of childish naivete. Yet, when Jesus first told people about that prayer and when people prayed to God in heaven, they were not thinking that the sky was totally irrelevant, or that the abode of God was in some kind of purely subjective realm. They saw the two as related. I think it's important to recover that sense of relationship between heaven in the traditional sense and the actual sky that we see.

We now have a view of the cosmos as a kind of developing organism. I think it's perfectly possible to think of the stars and galaxies and solar systems through the rest of the universe as having a life and intelligence of their own. In this way we can recover a sense of the life of the heavens, and presumably of an intelligence within the heavens, related perhaps to the traditional view of angels in some way.

There's also the question of the heavenly state which, in various traditions, is imagined in all sorts of ways. Christians and Muslims believe in the existence of heaven; I suppose Jews do too, although they're awfully vague and elusive when it comes to saying exactly what it is. The cartoon image of angels sitting on clouds playing harps gives us several indications: one, that it's dynamic, since clouds move; secondly, that it's not confined to normal laws of gravity—-otherwise the angel would sink through them; and thirdly, that it involves some kind of musical or vibratory nature. Among the different images of heaven, I've been very struck by Terence's descriptions of the state of mind induced by DMT (dimethyl tryptamine). This and perhaps other psychoactive substances can produce a state that in many ways resembles the state of heavenly bliss portrayed in religious literature.

I reject the idea of inner and outer in its usual sense. We're the victims of a humanistic culture that tells us that the whole of the external world is mere unconscious matter in motion, the province of the natural sciences. By contrast, religion, psychology and art are to do with the inner world, which implicitly is supposed to reside somewhere inside our brains and hence to decay when our brains decay. Heaven would in that case be something that you might enter through mystical states while you're alive, or drug states; certainly not somewhere you go when you die. I think the idea that inner states are actually inside our bodies is one of the false dichotomies set up by materialistic assumptions. I think that when we look around us, our minds are reaching out to fill the room or the place in which we are, and when we look at the stars, in some sense our mind reaches out to touch them. Although it's an inner perception to do with our psychology, the inner is actually outer as well. Therefore I take seriously the idea that heavenly states might be located at places other than inside our cerebral cortex or inside our bodies.

The vast majority of modern people know almost nothing about the heavens. Lots of people have books showing pictures of the earth from space, and children are given fantasy books about space travel. My own children, I am sad to say, learn more about the heavens from pictures of space ships than from looking at the sky. The actual sky is something of which most people are abysmally ignorant. In most traditional cultures people could recognize the stars. Mariners, shepherds, and ordinary people knew the basic constellations in the sky, and the planets.

This awareness of stars, the phases of the moon, and the general movements and positions of the planets, is widespread in traditional cultures. Of course the information is there in our culture, but it's hard to find someone who actually can point to the constellations in the sky. We are generally ignorant of the skies. The skies are now regarded from a scientific point of view as only matter, and that's the domain of astronomy. Oddly enough, even professional astronomers often don't know that much about the sky as we actually experience it, although they've got a lot of equations about the life cycle of stars, about the nature of pulsars and other strange mysteries in the heavens. I was having dinner a couple of years ago with the professor of astronomy in Britain. We went out after dinner. It was a beautiful starlit night. There was a group of stars I didn't know and I said, "What are those stars?" He said, "Oh I haven't a clue, don't ask me." He learned astronomy from books, from computer models, not from looking at the sky. A friend who works at the big observatory in Arizona told me his colleagues go inside and look through a big telescope at a particular star or galaxy, but if you ask them to point to it in the sky, they don't know. They just punch some figures into the computer to find it. They're not seeing the wood for the trees, or the sky for the stars. They don't see the bigger picture. Amateur astronomers and old-style celestial navigators are probably the only people who still keep alive the sense of observation and relationship to the heavens.

By contrast with the astronomers, astrologers have retained a sense of the heavens as meaningful, related to what happens on earth, but astrology has become detached from the actual sky. There's no use asking the average astrologer if you see a bright star in the sky or a planet, "What's that?" Most of them don't look at the sky anymore than other people. It's all done from computer programs and books. I was particularly struck in 1987, when there was a massive supernova in the Southern Hemisphere, the biggest since the one observed by Galileo and Kepler in 1604, which played a major part in the scientific revolution. All through history these supernovas—exploding stars in the sky—have been regarded as major omens of the greatest importance. I asked my astrologer friends, "What do you make of this?" The answer was they didn't make anything whatever of it because it wasn't in the ephemeris or in their Macintosh computer program. Astronomers, on the other hand, took great interest, but saw it with no meaning. I think a great move forward will happen when astronomy and astrology link up again.

I think much good will come from recovering a sense of the life of the heavens. We are coming to see the Earth, Gaia, as alive. I think we also have to take seriously the idea that the sun is alive and conscious. If one wants a scientific rationale for this, it comes ready to hand through the discoveries of modern solar physics. We now know that the sun has a complex system of magnetic fields, reversing its polarity every eleven years, associated with the sunspot cycle. With this underlying rhythm of magnetic polar reversals are a whole series of resonant and harmonic patterns of magnetic and electromagnetic change—global patterns over the surface of the sun of a fractal nature; patterns within patterns, highly turbulent, chaotic, sensitive, varied and complex. Electromagnetic patterns within our brains seem to be the interface between the mind and the nervous system, and here we have a comparable interface within the physical behavior of the sun. It's perfectly possible that the sun has a mind that interfaces with the complex activity we can observe.

The solar system itself is an organism. This is largely what astrology has concerned itself with. We also recognize that the sun is part of a galaxy, the Milky Way, which includes all the stars we see in the night sky. Like other galaxies, our own has a galactic center, a nucleus, of unknown nature which emits enormous amounts of radiation. We could think of galaxies as organisms as well. They come in clusters and these come in superclusters. These too can be thought of as organisms at higher levels of complexity and greater size. Our solar system is a tiny part of these vaster organisms within which it is embedded. If the sun has a kind of consciousness, what about the entire galaxy, with its mysterious center? What about galactic clusters? What about the cosmos as a whole?

Thus there may be levels of consciousness far beyond anything we experience ourselves, of ever more inclusive natures. When we turn to ancient traditions, we find that this has always been the general belief. The entire cosmos is believed to be animate. God is seen as residing beyond the sky but also in the sky: "Our Father who art in heaven." Although most modern people, including most educated Christians, assume that heaven doesn't mean the actual sky, I'd like us to entertain the notion that it does mean the sky. If God is omnipresent, then he must be present throughout the heavens, and since the heavens are vastly greater than the earth—about 99.99 recurring percent of the divine presence must be in the sky.

We can take the same crudely quantitative approach to arrive at the same conclusions about the celestial Goddess, who can also be seen as being or living in the heavens. In Egyptian mythology the sky was the abode of Nuit, the sky goddess, who was the womb of the heavens, and gave birth to the sun and the moon and the stars. She was the cause of space, the night skies, the womb from which all things come forth. That was the image also of Astarte, and that image has been assimilated into Christianity through the image of Mary, Mother of God, Queen of Heaven. For example, the form of Our Lady of Guadalupe is portrayed as wearing a sky-blue robe, studded with stars.

In Christian, Jewish, and Islamic belief there are various hierarchies of angels, usually nine. We could think of these celestial hierarchies as reflected in the super clusters of galaxies, galaxies, solar systems, suns and planets. The planets and the stars were traditionally believed to be the abodes of intelligent beings, and our English names for the planets are still those of classical gods and goddesses—Venus, Mercury, Mars, Jupiter, Saturn, and so on.

In the sixteenth century there was a revival of ancient star magic. In Elizabethan England, John Dee and others invoking the spirit of particular stars, asked for guidance, help and inspiration. It was an attempt to actually contact extraterrestrial intelligences, and communicate with them.

Ralph Abraham: The star magic idea in Elizabethan England preceded the nucleation of science as we know it, and represented a transmission from the ancient world, with a lot of changes, simplifications and additions. The central idea was the ancient notion of "The Great Chain of Being." In ancient Alexandria they liked to wrap up things in a package and send them into the future, and this idea actually reached us through the world of Islam. There were concentric spheres—nine, ten, or eleven, with the earth in the center. Outside of these spheres was nothing. The topmost sphere was the un-moving sphere of God and the other ones were of the planets and the sun and the moon, and they intermediated as midway stations in a kind of transmission, all the way from God down to us.

In Rome Giordano Bruno was burned at the stake on Easter Sunday in the year 1600 because he insisted on the infinity of the universe. He believed the stars were not on one sphere but outside the sphere of Jupiter, and that they filled all of space. The reason the church objected to this was that it left no space for God. Our Father in heaven had no place to go, and that was very threatening to the entire system.

I'm seeing in this cosmology you've presented an opportunity for us to construct a new cosmology of our own. A religion of the future could have a whole pantheon of gods and goddesses, including the living and sacred sun, moon, planets, Milky Way, quasars, nearby galaxies, clusters of galaxies, and so on.

I think the overall idea of a Great Chain of Being can be salvaged in our new cosmology without reference to our father god in heaven or even ideas of gods and goddesses and angels. The Search for Extraterrestrial Intelligence (SETI) would be a better description, because in our own journeys out of the body, we've sometimes left Earth far behind, reaching a realm difficult to name; transcendent, other; a realm well traveled by our forebears; brave travelers who have left all kinds of written records of their journeys. On our own journeys we've had the experience of meeting, conversing with, and being taught by extraterrestrial intelligences. Indeed our whole hope for the future is based somehow on these Gnostic experiences of direct contact with of extraterrestrial intelligence.

There may be a physical location in space and time, somewhere in the universe, for this intelligence; and there may not. Nevertheless, it's the conversation that is most important to us, not its identification with physical matter, energy or morphic fields. I'm not sure if I could connect an intelligent being I've encountered in out-of-body travel with the Milky Way or the planet Jupiter, although It makes sense to me when you say you believe they're intelligent beings. I can imagine the sunspots running across the face of the sun in furious speed as a kind of Cephalopod, octopus-like communication between one sun and another.

Terence McKenna: Are you saying that it's reasonable to connect up the entities in the psychedelic experience to particular places in space and time?

RA: Yes.

TM: It's hard for me to imagine that the sun is an intelligent organism, unless it exists on a scale that's fairly hard to relate to. In other words, I can imagine the Pacific Ocean to be intelligent, but its intelligence would be of such a nature that it and I probably wouldn't have much to do with each other. Meanwhile, out in the universe, somewhere, entities exist which we do contact in the psychedelic experience. I'm never sure if they're creatures of other levels or simply of other places. If other places, they seem to be so far away that the laws of physics are so different that it's not like the difference between

Chicago and Memphis, but like the difference between Chicago and Oz.

We've talked about how the morphogenetic field is a necessary hypothesis but hard to detect the way you can detect an electromagnetic field. The creative response is to hypothesize that perhaps the imagination is the detection equipment for the morphogenetic field. The brain-mind system is a quantum mechanically delicate enough chemical system that incoming input from the morphogenetic field can push cascades of chemical activity one way or another so that in the act of daydreaming or psychedelic tripping you're actually scanning the field. If that were the case, what we call the imagination is actually the universal library of what is real. This possibility, to me, is very empowering, and I suspect this is the truth you learn at the center of the psychedelic experience, that's so mind-boggling you can't really return to ordinary reality with it. If thinking about the heavens as organic, integrated, and animate makes this more probable, I'm all for it.

Rupert and I, and perhaps to some degree Ralph come out of the influence of a school of thought called Organismic Philosophy that was put forth by Alfred North Whitehead, Joseph Needham and L.L. Whyte. Rupert makes a very eloquent case for organismic organization at every level. The reason this is unwelcome in science is because it raises questions about the signal systems that hold these organisms together.

A machine communicates mechanical force basically through direct contact. An organism operates through chemical systems of diffusion, or color signal, or in some cases language. It's these higher-order forms of function, when called down to explain large chunks of nature, that begin to look like a reinfusion of spirit into nature. This is of course exactly what we need, although orthodoxy fights it tooth and nail in ongoing reaction to the nineteenth century battle where deism had the power to potentially frustrate Darwinian rationalism. It's time to realize that battle was won long ago, and that trying to reason upward from the laws of atomic physics to organisms is not going to work. There are what David Bohm calls "emergent properties," at every level. Think of a single molecule of water; it's absurd to call it wet. Wetness is an emergent property that comes out of millions of molecules of water. At every level in the evolution of physical complexity, complexity itself permits the emergence of new properties, with the iridescence of mind and culture emerging finally at the top of the pyramid.

It's interesting the way the culture has changed its attitude toward the heavens. One revolution in our thinking that is fairly fundamental is that no one at this point believes in the human conquest of space. This has gone from a national commitment in the '60s to the chic thing to be into in the '70s, to hardly being mentioned today, either by freaks like us, or presidential candidates, or right wingers, left wingers, middle-of-the-roaders or anybody else. It all seems to be over. The heavy lift launch capacity that resided in the Soviet military-industrial complex and that held the keys to reaching near earth orbit has been allowed to drift into obsolescence. I appreciate your attempt to animate the cosmos, because apparently we're turning away from it, having become a part of the past era of grandeur and glory, seeming not to be repeated.

We held a Virtual Reality conference at Esalen recently and Howard Rheingold had a revelation in the middle of the night down on the platform in front of the Big House when he said, "My God, now I understand what virtual reality is for! It's to keep us from ever leaving the Earth!"

RS: It seems to me, in terms of communication with other planets, the SETI program which is now based on radio telescopes and high technology won't get very far. There seem to be three points in favor of another approach. First, if we're trying to communicate with beings on our own level, i.e., biological organisms on planets somewhere else in the universe, it may be that shamanic journeys into the heavens, which are a long part of a very long tradition going on for hundreds of thousands of years, may already have contacted beings of a similar order to ourselves.

Second, there's the possibility of communication with a higher kind of mind or intelligence, like the Pacific Ocean, the Sun, the solar system, or the galaxy. Terence, I think you dismissed it too quickly. The idea that our minds are very much smaller parts of a very much larger mental system, incomprehensible to us because it's so much larger, working on different time scales, is of course a very traditional idea. We don't have to stay at our own level. Perhaps we can communicate with these higher levels of intelligence through prayer, mystical insight, or intuition. Most forms of mysticism today are extremely fuzzy because as soon as we get beyond the human level, we lack maps. When it comes to a sense of absorption into the nature of a place, or Gaia, or the solar system, or the galaxy, or the cluster of galaxies, or the cosmos, or the unifying spirit pervading the entire cosmos, most people don't quite know where one leaves off and the next begins. All they know is that all these things are bigger than them. It may be that in the past people had a better sense of just where they were going. The doctrine of hierarchies of angels was a way of recognizing that there are many different levels of intelligence or mind beyond our own.

The third point is that in order to contact extra-terrestrial intelligences, it may help to direct these efforts toward particular parts of the heavens. There are traditional beliefs about the qualities of particular stars, and these might provide a guide as to what to expect. Regulus, for example, in the constellation Leo, was considered a star of good omen. Looking at it, going into an altered state having invoked its spirit, making the appropriate prayers and preparations, could result in a form of directed mind travel that would go beyond random journeying. This would be a new frontier of space exploration that can be done on a very low budget. It could open up a great range of possibilities.

TM: I think it's a wonderful idea. I can envision using the Keck telescope, punching up *Algol* on the screen and then smoking DMT and putting your hand on the radio, as they used to say. It could work! I don't doubt it for a moment.

RA: I do know somebody who undertook a program like this. It was me actually. The technical equipment that made this project possible, empowering me to travel to my destination, the stars, was my hot tub, an instrument that makes it comfortable to sit outdoors for a long time watching the sky. I explored primarily the polar constellations and the Milky Way. I found that some kind of conversation with the Milky Way is possible, as well as with the Zodiac and the zodiacal constellations, particularly the lunar and solar constellations. They each have a lot to say about the morphic field.

I return to John Dee and his conversations with angels. Dee interpreted mathematics as being a healing art, in which the stellar influences could be used for healing human diseases. We could apply this idea on a larger scale, where our future and the biosphere's future are threatened. We could ask the Guardian Angel of the Anima Mundi, for example, to give aid in our planetary predicament by instructing us not as individual humans, but collectively as a human species. This was the program that I had in mind in my experiment. I was asking for guidance in a visual form—a vision of the kind that I've been struggling with machinery to reproduce. I've not so far received a solution to our problems, but I do think this is a program that an individual can pursue, even without psychedelics. It requires a considerable commitment of time.

RS: We can start nearer to home with the sun, of course. At sunrise and sunset in many traditions people have communicated with the sun. In India a traditional part of the daily ritual is to greet the sun as it rises in the morning, in order to form a conscious relationship with it. Our own civilization is based to an extraordinary degree on what's jocularly called "sun worship." Millions of people spend the winter fantasizing about which beach they're going to go to in the summer. This curious movement in our civilization toward a new relationship to the sun is relatively recent. In the nineteenth century very few people lay around in the sun.

RA: I think we should reconsider the moon. The Lunar Sphere, among the nine celestial spheres, is somehow the most important to us, as it's the membrane for our kind of life. The traditional idea was that everything inside the lunar sphere decays and dies, and everything outside the lunar sphere is eternal. The moon was somehow always seen as the boundary of mortal life. Furthermore, everyone loves to look at it, and probably love and the emotional structure of the human and mammalian system has evolved by moonlight. The moon might be our likeliest possibility for actually having a conversation and renewing our contact with the living and intelligent universe.

RS: I myself don't expect the moon to have a great deal of intelligence or life. It's the most inert heavenly body we know. Venus, on the other hand, is a turbulent system with plenty of scope for chaotic perturbations and shifting systems of order. Jupiter has this extraordinarily turbulent surface. Saturn has delicately poised and no doubt oscillatory rings many of them sensitive enough to pick up fleeting changes and act as interfaces between the physical and mental realms. The moon seems rather lacking in all of these respects.

RA: Okay, maybe the moon is dumb. I'm not willing to concede that, but I see that some people would rather put their money on a different number. Of the brighter planets, Jupiter is probably the one that most people are familiar with. Jupiter and Saturn are visible in the sky almost like stars. They stay in the same position for a long time, so it's easy to find them without a computer-controlled stellarator. So what about contacting Jupiter or Saturn?

TM: There's plenty of exotic chemistry on Jupiter. The current thinking is that Europa is the most likely place in the solar system other than the earth to have life, because of its very dense, deep oceans, filled with liquid water. It may be, in fact, that the entire thing is a drop of liquid water. There may be no solid form.

These other kinds of life I dare say live mostly in our fevered imaginations at this point. I mean the evidence for them is extraordinarily underwhelming I would think. The difficulty about this whole discussion about extraterrestrial intelligence, or nonhuman intelligence, is that the very nature of its nonhumanness makes it either elusive, uninteresting, or horrifying. It's probably in a very narrow spectrum that we can have the experience of an I-Thou relationship. We can decide here and now that in fact the sun is alive and highly literate and so forth. It doesn't greatly change our experience in the way that an extraterrestrial with which we could exchange information would. I think the recognition of intelligence if it's not like ours, is going to be very difficult. I mean we can't even have Croats and Serbs getting along together.

RA: But we've already encountered intelligence; let's call it the "Transcendent Other" for the moment. Suppose it turned out that the Transcendent Other was not in hyperdimensional space; in other words beyond space and time, living on the other side of the *Eschaton*, but actually lived in a crater on the moon. That would not only be an interesting discovery but would completely change your whole idea about shamanic experience.

TM: So far, the only locators we've been able to find for these things are drugs. In other words, we can say this creature lives on the other side of 15 milligrams of psilocybin, but not on the other side of 75 milliliters of ayahuasca. These may not be satisfying as locators because we're not used to thinking of molecules as standing for spatio-temporal locus.

RA: In John Dee's system, everything represented a planetary intelligence.

RS: If we're looking for guidance in what happens on Earth, and we certainly need it, we must recognize how we're imbedded within the heavens, the solar system, the galaxy, the cosmos. Intelligences throughout the heavens could play an important role in guiding us.

We are fascinated by our own death, although we deny it and transfer it onto larger spheres. Now that we've achieved more or less the largest sphere in our search for the eventual death of the all and everything, perhaps we could extend the same consideration to creativity and birth and see the acorn, growing into the mature tree, as the ultimate principle of life. In these seeds, birth moments are distributed everywhere in space and time and throughout the reality of the universe.

CHAPTER 11

THE END OF REALTY

Rupert Sheldrake: I'd like to read a part of the last letter I received from my teacher, Father Bede Griffiths. He was an English Benedictine monk who lived for nearly forty years in India. He died in 1993 at the age of 86 in his ashram on the bank of the Cauvery river in Tamil Nadu, South India. I lived in his community for two years; it's where I wrote my first book, *A New Science of Life*, which I dedicated to Father Bede.

His letter was written on All Souls' Day, November 2, 1992, in response to our book *Trialogues at the Edge of the West* (now published as *Chaos, Creativity and Cosmic Consciousness*).

My Dear Rupert,
I've just finished reading your Trialogues with Ralph and Terence. It is as near a map to the future that I

have ever encountered, embracing every aspect of life as it is understood today. The only thing I find lacking in it is a sense of the mystical, of the unity which transcends all dualities. Your view of apocalypse is very impressive, but one must remember that all time and space is contained in the transcendent unity which embraces all the multiplicity. The Tibetans see this very clearly. All the multiplicity of forms is a manifestation of the one formless reality. I think that David Bohm's idea of the implicate order is very meaningful.

RS: David Bohm, the quantum physicist, proposed that behind the world that we experience, the explicate order is an invisible, unmanifested source: the implicate order. Father Bede continues:

Chaos is the original undifferentiated unity, the prime matter of Aristotle, in which all forms are implicated. As consciousness emerges from the primal unity the different forms of being are gradually explicated. You can think of it as the emergence of form from the original chaos or the descent of form from the original spirit. Matter is form emerging from chaos; spirit is form in its original unity. In other words, matter is form emerging from the unconscious; spirit is form communicating itself to matter. Matter is the mother, the receptive principle (the yin), form is the father, the active principle (the yang). But all these principles are expressions of the differentiating consciousness, which itself is beyond differentia-

tion. So from an undifferentiated consciousness we pass to a differentiated consciousness. Consciousness divides, but only to reunite.

The danger is that we get stuck in the differentiated consciousness, which is where we are now. But all differentiation leads back to a unity which transcends differences. This is the final state of nirvana, sunyata, or nirguna Brahma, Brahma without qualities. In the Trinity everything comes from its original source in the Father beyond differentiation, and comes forth in the Son in all the multiplicity of the universe, and returns in the Spirit to the original transcendent unity, but now in full consciousness.

This is how I see it, but you bring an abundance of new insights from science, which are new to me. In regard to education I think that it's important to be based on traditional religion, whether Hindu, Christian, or American Indian. A tradition links you vitally with the past and enables you to grow. Of course, it can also prevent growth, but our call is precisely to allow the tradition to grow, and to be open to all the new insights which are offered us. But to start without roots in tradition I feel would be frustrating.

One point Father Bede is making is that in our first book we didn't speak much about the transcendent source Although in the course of our discussions over the years, we have referred to it repeatedly, particularly in what Terence says about the cosmic attractor. This unity which Father Bede refers to contains all multiplicity, because it contains all the variety of forms in creation. When he talks about the unity which transcends all dualities, this transcendent unity which embraces all multiplicity, it sounds to me very like what Terence is talking about at the end of time.

Terence McKenna: I agree. It's absolutely the same thing. I think that since the publication of *Trialogues at the Edge of the West*, we've tended more and more to address this precise issue. I don't have any problem with any of it. It's certainly part of the picture.

Ralph Abraham: I'm not sure we'll ever get finished discussing this point. My own views of the mystical and the unity of phenomena in the world are still evolving. Actually, our interaction in our discussions continues to present different views about the details of this picture of the connectedness of all and everything. More specifically, I think our recent discussions have had the function of decreasing dualism somehow, especially in our discussions about the heavens. When we talked about the location of heaven from a real-estate perspective, we arrived at a kind of integration into a unity of all and everything. As I listened to our discussion, I imagined a unity of the dualism of form and matter and energy, not only unified in a primal cause, or primal *Eschaton*, but through all time. In the present moment as well, there is the interaction of matter and spirit within the integrity of a single phenomenon or trans-temporal object. Even now the entelechy, or causal phenomenon, has a concept of time in it, which I think is more specific and special than, for example Brahma, the unity of all and everything—the spirit and the world in one.

We tried to integrate heaven and Earth in our discussion by locating a door to the paranormal dimensions at each and every point in ordinary space and time. This is a kind of time-less integration in which the whole of time becomes a kind of slice in this trans-temporal causal object. This is a little bit different, as I see it, from the idea of the *Eschaton*, the attractor at the end of time.

RS: This is the holographic matrix, all-in-everything model.

TM: It assumes that the higher, trans-temporal dimension can be accessed from anywhere in space and time. I suppose this is like the difference between individual and collective salvation, as one must believe that the individual at any point can truncate the process and cut to the chase, although clearly the species is locked in a larger drama that has to unfold according to its own dynamics before it's completed.

RA: I agree that ordinary reality lives in space and time, and the individual subjective experience of time is exactly what it seems to be. From the individual perspective, the model, the master form, chaos, can be visualized within ordinary reality either at the beginning of time or the end of time. A truly transcendental vision sees time as a kind of lower-dimensional phenomenon in the all-embracing picture of the overall unity of reality.

RS: "Time is the moving image of eternity," in Plato's words in the *Timaeus*.

RA: And eternity is not at the end of time.

RS: I think we've run into a problem, because all the Platonic formulations are based on a cyclical view of the universe. Whereas the evolutionary view, which is Whitehead's view and Terence's view and my own view, are based on a different model of time, namely time as a development or movement towards an end or a goal. Because of evolutionary theory, the attempts in the twentieth century of theologians and philosophers to grapple with the problem of the eternity and unity of time have been different from the problems faced by their predecessors. Teilhard de Chardin tried to adapt traditional theology to the evolutionary view and in India, Sri Aurobindo put forth a similar evolutionary idea.

It's one thing to have the image of a transcendent reality that generates endless cycles of recurrence: the great breath of Brahma, the Great Year, and that kind of thing. It's another thing to have a model where the whole thing is developing toward a *telos*, an end, goal or cosmic attractor. This evolutionary view, which is fundamental to my own thinking, depends on an asymmetry in time, an increasing diversity of forms and the appearance of novelty as well. All these things are difficult to square with traditional theologies.

If you have the idea of cycles, then the transcendent and the temporal exist in some kind of ongoing, more or less eternal relationship. Time, as the moving image of eternity, goes round and round in circles, which is the closest approximation of eternal movement that the Greeks or anyone else could come up with. This is not the evolutionary version, where time moves increasingly faster and faster, as Terence tells us, towards some kind of cosmic culmination.

This has been a problem in Christian theology right from the beginning, because on the one hand the Christians inherited Greek Neo-Platonic philosophy. On the other hand, deep within the Judeo-Christian tradition is the idea of a process in time moving towards a culmination, an apocalypse, the *Eschaton*, the Messiah, the Second Coming, the Millennium. This tension has become exacerbated in this century because we've taken so seriously the evolutionary view, with its implication of a movement of things towards an end, a culmination, a goal. We now see the whole universe and life and human development under the aspect of evolutionary development. Previously, the idea was that the universe is more or less static once created, or cycling endlessly, with human beings engaged in this endless process.

RA: I wish that Father Bede were here to instruct us. I interpret his words to mean that the evolutionary or linear-progressive model is actually a denial of the mystical vision that he presents. Eric Voegelin described history, the past and the future, as radiating symmetrically from the present. Rather than locating the *Eschaton* in the present and considering evolution both ways, I would think it's possible to envision time as an endless line. If time is thus regarded asymmetrically, where the past is considered to be more determined than the future, then today's efforts will matter in the long run.

The space-time model of ordinary reality can still be seen in its entirety as an arena for the morphogenetic process, which stretches over all and gives us the asymmetry of ordinary perception of the process. This reconciles the model of evolution with the growth of the morphogenetic field and so on.

Nevertheless, there's interconnectedness between the past, the present and the future, as part of a morphogenetic process stretching over the entire space-time continuum. It's possible that pattern formation in the past is still taking place as we perceive it in the present. When we do archaeology we reconstruct the past, much as when we try to remember what we did or said yesterday, remembering selectively, introducing errors, which progress each day to different errors and so on. As far as consciousness is concerned, there's a morphogenesis over the whole space-time continuum. In this context, we can unify the mystical view of the all and everything with the concept of linear evolution.

TM: However, I don't think Father Bede would abandon orthodoxy, and the distinguishing characteristic of Western orthodoxy, whether Judaism, Christianity or Islam, is the absolute and uncompromised assurance that God will enter history at a certain moment. That's the distinguishing characteristic of Western, as opposed to Eastern religion.

RS: Not will, but has entered history.

TM: And will again. It's a promise that must be redeemed, and it's completely counterintuitive, completely antirational. It makes far less sense than the endless cycling of Hinduism or the quietism of Taoism. There is an irrational insistence at the heart of Western religion, and I don't think it will ever be traded away.

RS: There's a fundamental asymmetry in our conception of time, built into the system from which Father Bede is speaking.

TM: Exactly. People forget, for example, that as recently as the early twentieth century Arnold Toynbee wrote a study of history in which he states that the culmination of history is the entry of God into three-dimensional space. This is considered modern historiography done in the Western tradition.

RS: There are two things one can say to that. First, in most esoteric formulations of the Christian view there is the entry of God at the end of time. In the more mystical view you have the idea of the entry of God all the time, in the lives of all believers. In this view, people are always potentially open to the spirit, because the spirit is that which is inspiring, dynamical, moving; it's the novelty wave, if you like, because it's that which causes change. The Christian view is not that God is undifferentiated; there's always a trinity of Spirit, and Father, and the Logos or the Son, existing in relationship. The part of the trinity that's a moving principle, the spirit, is always conceived of in moving images; as the breath, the wind, the fire, the flame, the flight of the bird. These movements are not predictable, at least in any ordinary sense. Jesus says to Nicodemus in John's Gospel, "The wind bloweth where it listeth, and thou hearest the sound thereof, but canst not tell whence it cometh, and whither it goeth; so is everyone that is born of the Spirit" (John 3:8). The idea is that the spirit is inherently unpredictable, a moving principle, present in all people, all of nature and containing the element of surprise. There's also the formal principle, the Logos, which gives things their form. The Logos evolves as creation evolves, and there's always this dynamical Spirit within it.

There's a sense in which the Christian view has never been particularly compatible with the Platonic view, or with an ex-

treme monotheism, which has an undifferentiated, changeless, eternal unity, outside time. The Holy Trinity has process
within it, the Spirit being the breath, the Word being the spoken word.

Alfred North Whitehead, of whom you often speak, Terence, was not only a great philosopher, but he also founded
one of the most interesting schools of twentieth-century theology. His father was an Anglican vicar, and he himself was
extremely preoccupied with questions of theology. His view of
reality as process led him to a new interpretation of the divine
process, and to the establishment of a school of evolutionary
theology, called Process Theology. It leads to the idea of the
evolutionary process as some kind of divine process, a manifestation of the divine process working itself out through creation. Therefore there is a sense in which God evolves. Process
theologians talk of two poles of the divine: one an eternal pole,
which is changeless; the other an evolutionary pole, always
changing. Somehow these poles come together in a final culmination.

With this view we get a much greater sense of the evolutionary process on Earth and in the whole cosmos as part of
the divine process, not somehow external to it. Actually, the
speaking of the Word, the vibratory coming forth of things in
time can be seen as the very essence of the divine nature. This
is partly what Matthew Fox means by the Cosmic Christ.
When St. John says at the beginning of his gospel, "In the beginning was the Word," he doesn't mean in the beginning was
Jesus of Nazareth. He means that in the beginning was the
cosmic creative process with consciousness, meaning, and a
vibratory nature. "Word" implies a process in time, with a be-

ginning, middle and end. The whole universe is, in a sense, the Cosmic Christ, a divine, creative cosmos.

RA: That's what I meant by the space-time model of reality: the space-time continuum with all phenomena attached, including individual consciousness, the morphogenetic field, the wave functions of quantum mechanics, and the extra dimensions of the image, and so on. We could just call it the Logos and avoid the word "Word" because of its habitual association with sound and the lower-dimensional languages.

RS: I think it's better to keep that association, because sound and "Word" have the same sense of beginning and end.

RA: As you like. This sensorium of God is very compatible with the view of general relativity and of quantum mechanics, where the functions describing ordinary reality and perceptions are distributed over the whole of space and time, and vibrations in the past are still ringing into the future and vice versa. From this perspective you have what can be viewed as an evolutionary equation in which not only the curvature of space, but also the very topology of space, including black holes, worm holes, and so on, is evolving in time. On the other hand, if you impress any kind of boundary condition, like a hypothesis of the future, or a hypothesis of the past, onto the picture, then the possible topology in this evolution is severely restricted.

What you're suggesting is very consistent with the modern scientific view of the universe. This could be interpreted as an evolution of cosmology as well, but we have a different picture of the mystical unity now than we did previously. Still, there seems to me to remain a tension between the idea of linear progress and the asymmetry of time on the one hand and the mystical view of the union of things. Even the entry of God into the model, can be thought of as a zipper that's unzipped and connected only at the ends. God intervenes here and there; meanwhile, humans and other creatures are free to screw up as much as they want.

On the other hand, the idea of the perpetual intervention of God suggests a knitting together of things in a more holistic way. The zipper is zipped, and consciousness is totally inter-connected at all times. I think these are two entirely different views. The idea that you described under the name Process Theology seems particularly consistent with the modern view.

From the perspective of chaos theory, I think that the emergence of form from chaos in the morphogenetic process can be viewed either within the linear progression of time, or outside of it. I prefer to think of it as being connected through-out time, and that the linear progress of time is some kind of illusion that's normal for biological life.

RS: It's not exactly linear; it's developmental. One way of rep-resenting this is through the idea of entelechy, which draws a living organism toward an end or goal. As Aristotle said, the entelechy of the oak tree draws the acorn toward the mature form of the oak. This process can be disturbed—insects eat the leaves, lightning strikes it, branches are blown off in a storm, there may be a long drought—all these accidents can happen. The exact course of its development is not exactly predictable, but the entelechy continues to draw it toward its mature form, enabling it to regenerate after damage. Unless it's killed off, it inexorably continues its development.

Another way of representing the evolutionary process is through the idea of an attraction that lures creation toward some kind of completion or culmination, as some process theologians would express it. This cosmic end or goal is what Teilhard de Chardin called the Omega Point. Terence calls it the cosmic attractor. Freedom, diversions, digressions, and all sorts of things can happen on the way, but there's some kind of attractor towards which it's all being pulled. This seems to me entirely consistent with the traditional Christian view, although Terence puts it across more forcibly than most of the professional proponents of Christianity. And more persuasively.

RA: Naturally I like these dynamical metaphors referring to the lure of attractors and so on; but in the perspective of the developmental aspect of time, there are in the dynamics of process and history certain moments of bifurcation. In a dynamical metaphor, bifurcation can be the time when the lure of the entelechy passes a moment of indeterminacy. In such a moment the intervention of God may be most appropriately attached to these dynamical events. A bifurcation in history such as the Renaissance is a time when anything can happen, and we don't know exactly what's going to evolve.

In chaotic dynamical systems, bifurcations can come in fractal clusters, which are called fractal bifurcation events. That means that you have something like a Cantor set of bifurcation moments creating zones of indeterminacy that fill up a fairly large amount of time. In other words, the moments occur very frequently when the intervention of God or even of human will affect history—even during a single day.

TM: It sounds like the time wave.

RA: Exactly. This is a punctuation of the whole entelechy concept, where Aristotle fails and Plato succeeds. There's so
much flexibility in this process, as viewed in the content of the
dynamical metaphor, that the acorn that Aristotle refers to,
could become a tree with five limbs or a tree with three limbs.
There are a lot of variations that occur even within the micro-
structure of time, as in the microsecond timing of cellular
events and so on. This variability fractally permeates the entire structure of time and the divine regulation of events. It actually liberates us from the simple notion of entelechy, the
lure of a final destiny of the process.

RS: There's a great deal of freedom, within constraints. In the
oak tree, the vein pattern in every leaf is different, and it's different on the two sides of the same leaf.

RA: But it's still an oak tree.

RS: And each leaf is still an oak leaf; but if you look at the pattern of veins in a leaf, this is literally a primordial image of bifurcation. In the branching of the veins you have a different
pattern in every leaf, while the overall general structure is
similar. You can tell it's an oak tree and not a beech tree at a
glance.

RA: If the morphogenetic field is thought of as stretched over
the whole of time, with some special spotlight on the present
movement, then the development of a mature oak tree with an
indeterminate number of leaves is already projected onto the

future in a probabilistic way. The oak tree forms the successive concretization of this probability wave, as the spotlight of time moves along. From the point of the view of the mystical unity, these fields do extend over the whole of time, even if it's infinitely in the past and in the future.

TM: The important thing to keep in mind is that the whole of time is probably not the same thing as forever.

RS: That would follow from the idea of entelechy, a culmination towards which animate beings move. The only way to get to forever is to link on a new cycle at the end.

RA: Right.

RS: Let's say the oak tree has acorns and it starts all over again; the universe gives rise to baby universes, which begin again. This is not a question within our own universe, which by definition is a unity: a "uni-verse" rather than a "multi-verse." If our universe has an attractor, a universal process, then we can leave open the question as to whether there's another one after it. There's a culmination, the universe comes to flower, to maturity; but in the details of evolution, we get galaxies, stars, plants, molecules, crystals, fish, camels, and so on, a vast variety of forms. There's a lot of freedom in the evolutionary process, including the human evolutionary process. Things could be otherwise.

Despite all Terence's efforts, human beings may not make it. The year 2012 may be the human moment of truth; but it may not be the cosmic moment of truth, or even the moment of truth for life on this Earth. Terence's map is based on human history, and it may be that if humans blow it, then 2012 will simply mark the collapse of civilization, mass catastrophes, famines, civil wars in epidemic proportions, human beings reduced to a few scattered bands of survivors . . .

RA: And microbes will begin again.

RS: Or herrings, squirrels, and many other kinds of animals and plants. They may have their own version of the time wave and of evolution. Terence's evidence refers only to human history. Apart from a few asides about the sun and neutrinos, it leaves out most of the cosmos. It may be that the time wave leads to a culmination of our species, while another kind of time wave would apply to the evolution of other species. There may also be a time wave that applies to the entire cosmos. For this reason it's worth looking at astronomical indicators like variations in sun spot cycles or the occurrence of supernovae, exploding stars, which are presumably intense vortices of novelty. We could look at the occurrence of supernovae through the universe and derive some index of the distribution of novelty in time and space on a cosmological scale.

TM: The clustering of galaxies themselves in deep wells of space represents aggregations of novelty that are orders of magnitude more complex than the empty space between them. Since the discovery of the great attractor, it can be reasonably said that every phenomenon observable in the universe is furiously moving toward something, under the attraction of some larger system. There are whole groups of galaxies bound together by attractive forces, and planetary systems, human social systems, atomic subsystems, all bound to their local attractor and being pumped through the whole, as a subset of these larger attractive processes.

RA: This means that rather than thinking of the *Eschaton* as a big bang, or the culmination of all of the consciousness of the universe, we can see the entelechy as distributed in time. The human species can have its Omega Point at a particular moment in the time scale of the universe, while the nuclear process of the sun has its Omega Point and the solar system has its Omega Point. Considering all the different scales of the perceived universe, these could be distributed in time and space, so we can say that there's entelechy everywhere, each comprising its own space-time continuum of extraordinary reality. This distributed model of entelechy itself would be a kind of a wave function, with its own time and novelty waves and its own probability functions and morphogenetic fields and so on. In this way we can get away from the particle view of entelechy and into the wave spectrum, a new kind of model of the universe.

Freud describes this strange fascination with entelechy and the *Eschaton* as a manifestation of Thanatos. We are fascinated by our own death, although we deny it and transfer it onto larger spheres. Now that we've achieved more or less the largest sphere in our search for the eventual death of the all and everything, perhaps we could extend the same consideration to creativity and birth and see the acorn, growing into the mature tree, as the ultimate principle of life. In these seeds, birth moments are distributed everywhere in space and time and throughout the reality of the universe.

SELECTED READINGS

The authors have referred to these readings in their conversations in the designated chapters.

CHAPTER ONE

Barbara Erhrenreich, *Blood Rites: Origins and History of the Passions of War* (New York: Henry Holt and Company LLC, 1997)

Stephen Mithen, *The Prehistory of the Mind: The Cognitive Origins of Art, Religion and Science* (London: Thames and Hudson Ltd., 1996)

Steven Pinker, *How the Mind Works* (New York: W. W. Norton, 1997).

Rupert Sheldrake, *The Presence of the Past: Morphic Resonance & the Habits of Nature* (New York: Times Books, 1988).

CHAPTER TWO

Hans Jenny, *Kymatik Cymatics* (Basel: Basileus Press, 1974)

Terence McKenna, *The Archaic Revival: Speculations on Psychedelic Mushrooms, the Amazon, Virtual Reality, UFOs, Evolution, Shamanism, the Rebirth of the Goddess, and the End of History* (San Francisco: HarperSanFrancisco, 1992)

Terence McKenna, *Food of the Gods: The Search for the Original Tree of Knowledge, A Radical History of Plants, Drugs, and Human Evolution* (New York: Bantam, 1992)

Marshall McLuhan, *The Gutenberg Galaxy: The Making of Typographic Man* (Toronto: University of Toronto Press, 1962)

Marshall McLuhan, *Understanding Media: The Extensions of Man* (Cambridge, MA: The MIT Press; Reprint edition (October 20, 1994)

Rupert Sheldrake, *The Rebirth of Nature* (New York: Bantam, Reprint edition (April 1, 1992)

CHAPTER THREE

Hans Alfven, *Worlds-Antiworlds: Antimatter in Cosmology* (San Francisco: W.H. Freeman, 1966).

Kurt Gödel, *The Consistency of the Axiom of Choice* (Princeton: Princeton University Press, 1940)

Giorgio de Santillana and Hertha Von Dechend, *Hamlet's Mill: An Essay on Myth and the Frame of Time* (David R. Godine Publisher; Reissue edition, 1992)

Immanuel Velikovsky, *Worlds in Collision* (New York: Amereon Limited, 1999)

C.H. Waddington, *The Nature of Life* (London: Allen and Unwin, 1961)

CHAPTER FOUR

Rupert Sheldrake, *Seven Experiments that Could Change the World* (London: Fourth Estate, 1994).

CHAPTER FIVE

Norman Cohn, *The Pursuit of the Millennium: Revolutionary Millenarians and Mystical Anarchists of the Middle Ages* (New York: Oxford University Press, Revised and expanded edition, 1990)

Riane Eisler, *The Chalice and the Blade: Our History, Our Future* (San Francisco: HarperSanFrancisco, 1988)

Frank E. Manuel and Fritzie Prigohzy Manuel, *Utopian Thought in the Western World* (Cambridge, Mass.: Harvard University Press, 1982)

Paul Tillich, *Political Expectation* (New York: Harper & Row, 1971)

Delno C. West and Sandra Zimdars-Swartz, *Joachim of Fiore: A Study in Spiritual Perception and History* (Bloomington: Indiana University Press, 1983).

CHAPTER SEVEN

Rupert Sheldrake, *Dogs That Know When Their Owners Are Coming Home, And Other Unexplained Powers of Animals* (New York: Three Rivers Press, 2000)

CHAPTER EIGHT

Terence Kealey, *The Economic Laws of Scientific Research* (New York: St. Martin's Press, 1996)

CHAPTER NINE

Plotinus, *The Enneads*, trans. by Stephen MacKenna (Burdett, N.Y: Larson Publications, 1992)

CHAPTER TEN

Terence McKenna, *The Archaic Revival: Speculations on Psychedelic Mushrooms, the Amazon, Virtual Reality, UFOs, Evolution, Shamanism, the Rebirth of the Goddess, and the End of History* (San Francisco: HarperSanFrancisco, 1992)

Rupert Sheldrake, *The Rebirth of Nature* (New York: Bantam, Reprint edition, 1992)

CHAPTER ELEVEN

Ralph Abraham, Terence McKenna and Rupert Sheldrake, *Chaos, Creativity and Cosmic Consciousness* (Rochester, VT: Park Street Press, 2001).

Aurobindo (Sri), *The Life Divine* (Twin Lakes, WI: Lotus Press, 1985)

David Bohm, *Wholeness and the Implicate Order* (London: Routledge and Kegan Paul, 1980)

Pier Teilhard de Chardin, *The Phenomenon of Man* (New York: Perennial Classics, 1976)

Matthew Fox, *The Coming of the Cosmic Christ* (San Francisco: HarperSanFrancisco, 1988)

Rupert Sheldrake, *A New Science of Life* (Rochester, VT: Park

Street Press, Reprint edition, 1995)

Alfred North Whitehead, *Process And Reality* *(Gifford Lectures Delivered in the University of Edinburgh During the Session 1927-28)* (New York: Free Press, Corrected edition, 1979)

CPSIA information can be obtained at www.ICGtesting.com
Printed in the USA
LVOW09s0803050215

425815LV00001B/1/P